My Name Is Innocent

To Gena + Katie —
Fellow ministers in
God's rich field.

Dale Freeman

Library of Congress Catalog Card Number 95-68800

ISBN Number 1-57087-145-0

Production design by Robin Ober

Professional Press
Chapel Hill, NC 27515-4371

Manufactured in the United States of America
96 95 94 93 92   10 9 8 7 6 5 4 3 2 1

For Dr. C. E. Autrey
Beloved mentor, encourager,
and father in the ministry.

"The meeting of two personalities is like the contact of two chemical substances: if there is any reaction, both are transformed."

– C. G. Jung

Contents

Introduction 1

One   "My Name Is Innocent" 5

Two   Jimmy Hodges – Birth of a Vision 15

Three   True Tales of Africa 43

            "Behold What God Hath Done . . ." 43

            The Valley of Death 44

            The Sacrifice Tree 54

            Love Song 61

            Blind Allegiance 65

            The Appointment 69

            School Days 75

            The Frog Prince 81

Four   Malawi Journal 87

            "Miles To Go Before I Sleep . . . ." 88

            "Further Into The Night . . . ." 90

            "Our Destination" 91

            "The Pastors Arrive . . ." 92

            "Into The Harvest . . ." 94

            "Peddle Into All The World . . ." 97

            "Crusade!" 98

            "The Immensity Of It All!" 100

            "Cry For The Children" 101

            "Crusade Conclusion" 103

            "Harvest Thoughts" 104

            "The Greatest Adventure" 105

Five   The Message 107

Introduction

I had known Jimmy Hodges for several years. We had worked together in an evangelistic ministry, preaching the Gospel and singing His praises across the nation. I had since returned to the pastorate, and was ministering in the rapidly growing Denver metro area.

The Jimmy Hodges that sat across from me in the Peppermill Restaurant was different than the one I had traveled with. He had always brought a deep commitment, a love for souls and a wondrous talent to the Lord's service. But now, a new light glowed behind his dancing eyes.

He shared with me a unique vision that God had given him. The vision of a ministry that would allow leaders in Africa to be trained and inflamed so that they could be more effective in reaching their own continent for Christ. It would also provide an opportunity for Christians in the U.S. to help in the training process, and sometimes even be on location while thousands responded to the Gospel.

He was preparing to organize his first Institute for National Pastors and Evangelists in Kenya. The event would be held at the Brackenhurst Baptist International Conference Center in Limuru, a small community nestled in the mountains above the capital city of Nairobi. Pastors would be brought in for intensive training, and then would be taken into the streets, being taught first-hand in evangelism, witnessing and discipline. He wanted me to be the Director of this first event, and to lead one of the evangelism teams.

His vision gripped me, and the Lord stirred my heart. A few weeks later, I determined that it was God's purpose that I accept the invitation. I didn't realize that it was the first step in dramatically changing my life and ministry forever.

There, in the heart of Africa, God broke my heart and I discovered the world. I had been called to preach at age 16, had begun pastoring at age 21, and had been involved in ministry all of my adult life. I had led my churches to be committed to missions but I learned in Africa that I had known little about what I was doing. It would never be the same after Nairobi, and every priority and decision since that time has been impacted by those glorious days. It has been both my humble pleasure and delight to go again and again into that arena.

I write this book for several reasons. Most of all, I want to convey to you a slight glimpse of the wonders that God is performing around the world. I've broken the book down into several sections.

One part of the book is dedicated to the life and ministry of Jimmy Hodges. It was God's working through him that created a unique ministry that is shaking a continent. Only eternity will be able to reveal the countless souls that have been won through this work.

One section contains true stories of personal experiences that have taken place during some of these ministry projects. The names of U.S. personnel have been changed. My reason is simple. It really doesn't matter who was involved. The fact is that all of the miracles and blessings are attributed to God alone. While everyone involved is thankful for the opportunity, all will agree that none of these things could have taken place without the dynamic action of our Lord.

A final section is a portion of a Journal that I kept during the project in Blantyre, Malawi. It gives a sense of immediacy, and I trust that it'll help to take you even more personally into the center of the action.

So, lean back and read these few pages of true testimony. Marvel with us as we reflect on the grace of our Lord! Give Him all honor and glory as you rejoice at the report of lives and nations changed by the precious Gospel we have been given to proclaim!

Dale Freeman

One

"My Name Is Innocent"

*T*he noontime sun was unusually hot as I leaned against the smooth surface of the van. We had found a square island of dust and clay centered in the heart of Blantyre, the largest city in the Central African nation of Malawi.

We had passed all of the recognizable landmarks on our way to the Crusade site including the Mount Soche Hotel, just around the corner from the equally refined Ryall's Hotel.

Beyond these taller structures lay Blantyre's main shopping area filling a triangle that is tightly bordered by Victoria Avenue, Haile Selassie Road and the Glyn Jones Road. We had traveled down Victoria Avenue, passing various shops, banks, and the main PTC supermarket. Outside the PTC, facing a side road, was a covered section specially designed for the sale of curios. There, on the broken sidewalk, various wares were laid on mats for display, clever hawkers roaming around them, seeking to barter with anyone who looked remotely like they might have a little money.

Our vacant field was nearby, populated by only a few merchants, squatting on mats beneath the scattered shade provided by nearby trees. We had set up the site, parking the van and pickup in position, arranging the sound system and preparing the counseling materials for the Crusade service.

This event promised to be much different from those that we had conducted the day before. At that time, deep in the heart of the tea plantations of the country, we had settled into a series of meetings that allowed time to sing and visit with the people who had gathered. This city environment, amid whitewashed buildings filled with business people, demanded a much more direct approach. We would have to do our music, preaching and counseling within the sixty minutes that comprised the "lunch hour" for the workers. If anyone was to listen to us today, they would have to go without a meal.

The music had played, the crowd had gathered, and I retreated to the back of the site, listening to the testimonies and the beginning of the sermon. The week had been long, and I was beginning to feel the miles. We had seen a tremendous move of God in the hearts of the pastors we had trained at the Conference, and it was now becoming obvious that we were going to see a record number of people step forward to embrace Jesus.

Although I had been to Africa many times, I never ceased to be amazed. The simple proclamation of the Gospel was always accompanied by a sweeping move of God's Spirit. You could almost see the light of hope ignite behind the eyes of the people as you preached. Hearts melting, spirits embracing eternal truth. It had almost become commonplace to watch hundreds step forward at every invitation, kneeling to pray and receive the message.

"Sir."

A voice broke into my deliberations. I turned to be confronted by a thin lad of about 12, his arms wrapped tightly around a bundle of newspapers that he was obviously selling.

"Sir . . . Where are you from?"

"We're from the U.S.A.," I smiled. "We've come a long way to tell the people here in Blantyre good news."

The boy smiled, his bright eyes dancing. "Would it be possible for you to pray for me?" He stepped forward, leaning against the coarse rope that had been tied between our vehicles.

"Surely," I replied. "What can I do for you?"

"My name is Innocent." He paused for a long moment. "I speak English . . . but it's hard to say what I want." His eyes wandered across the field filled with people. He chose his words carefully.

"My heart is on fire," he breathed. "I would have Jesus as Lord. Will you pray with me?"

I moved forward and wrapped my arms around his shoulders. "Your name is Innocent?" He nodded positively. "You're really not, you know."

He looked startled. "Yes sir . . . I am."

"Innocent means 'without blame'. The Bible tells us that none of us are without blame. The Bible says that we have all sinned . . . we have all missed the mark . . . we've all fallen short of God's purpose for us. It's called sin . . . and that sin separates us from God and His Kingdom. It leads us to death."

"Then . . . what is this good news?"

"We can be forgiven . . . we can come alive to God and all that He is. We can invite Jesus into our lives, because God loved us so much that He sent His Son to pay the price for our sins and offer us a way of escape,"

I took my Bible from the front seat of the van, carefully leading him through several verses, watching his hungry eyes devouring each line. We prayed there, and I heard his soft voice expressing the surrender that was taking place in his heart.

"Fill out this card," I said. I gave him a decision card and he carefully printed his name and address. "Some people from a church here will get in touch with you. There are many more wonderful things that you need to know about God's love and His will for your life. They'll help you learn about these things."

He smiled, grasped my hand tightly and then walked away, turning to wave several times before he finally disappeared around the corner of the bustling market.

"It was like some Divine appointment," I whispered. I had shared my meeting with Innocent with many on the team. Now, sitting across from Jimmy Hodges, I once again told the story.

"It was like an affirmation of your vision for Africa," I said. "I believe that this young man may be called to preach the Gospel to his people. He may be leading Africa to Christ long after we're all dead and gone to Glory."

Jimmy smiled. We had been on such projects together many times, and he had learned that I was always looking for some direct intervention by the Lord. "You mean . . . reaching Africans to reach Africans."

"Yea . . . your vision. We're not going to reach Africa for Christ. Oh, sure . . . thousands come to the Lord in our Crusades, but the real payoff comes after we've gone back home.

It's the investment that we're making in the people here that's paying off the greatest dividends!"

"This young man means a lot to you, doesn't he?"

Jim had looked more deeply into my heart. He sensed the emotion behind my telling of the tale. I had already seen thousands accept Jesus during this week. Why such excitement over one young man?

"Yea . . . I needed him. The Lord knew it, and He arranged the appointment. You get lost in the masses sometimes. It happened to the disciples. They always saw the thousands and Jesus always saw the 'ones.' It's always the individual with Jesus! Maybe they come a thousand at a time . . . but He loves them and draws them to Himself . . . one by one by one."

"We have seen Him move in the masses alright." Jim always seemed surprised and amazed when he talked about God's moving through the frail labors of the teams.

"I needed just one. One to talk to . . . to put my arms around . . . to invest myself and some of my hopes in."

We sat in the dying light, listening to the jumbled chatter of the African men washing the vans and preparing them for the next day's crusades. We realized that neither one of us could explain why God had allowed us to be a part of it. But, we understood that He was doing it all . . . and we simply took another opportunity to thank Him for His grace and blessing.

I stepped into the gathering shadows, directing my steps toward my room and a short nap before the next appointment.

"Hello, sir." The familiar voice greeted me.

There, sitting on the low wall outlining the Lodge, was the boy named Innocent.

"What are you doing here?"

He smiled. "I must learn much more about God, and I want to be with the people who tell others."

I went to get him a Bible. We talked and prayed together again. "How did you find us, Innocent?"

He smiled sheepishly. "I asked a certain man in the city where I would find the people sent by God." He paused, carefully choosing his words. "That man sent me here to you."

The following day I loaded Innocent into the back of the truck with the national pastors and translators that were working with my team.

"I want to minister with you," he had told me. "I want to tell others of this wonderful thing that I now know."

We rumbled across rutted roads for almost an hour, finally positioning our trucks beneath an old tree mere feet from a teeming market place. Innocent helped with the equipment and was soon clapping his hands to the methodical beat of the music drawing people to the scene.

A lone man wandered around the perimeter of the service, his eyes glazed, his hands extended with waving fingers. "He is deaf and dumb," Innocent said. "He doesn't understand what is happening, and it is upsetting to him." He picked up a tract and moved through the crowd, welcoming the man and drawing him to a sitting position beneath the tree.

With patience and kindness the boy led the man through the book, sharing with him about the joy that comes through faith in Christ. Finally, with heads bowed, they prayed together, inviting a new reality into the searcher's heart and life.

Innocent returned to my side, the completed decision card in his hand. "He just needed to be told carefully," the boy mused. "I will go and tell others now."

He witnessed for the remainder of the day. Children, fellow young men and older adults yielded to his simple presentation of God's message, and many more were born into the Kingdom.

Innocent greeted me every day thereafter, walking with me through the streets of the city at every opportunity. I tried to teach him all that I could about his new life. The importance of the new Bible that he grasped in his hand, the reality of prayer that could usher him at any instant into God's unlimited presence, and the commission that he had so enthusiastically responded to.

"I believe that God has called me to take this message to my people," he confided. He would get no argument from me.

Finally, after the long days of labor in the field had concluded, we were packing the trucks and preparing for our long journey home. Innocent stood in the early morning light, watching our efforts. He had been sitting on the porch of the lodge since sunrise, waiting for the time of departure.

"Innocent . . . I'm going to send you a book when I get home. It'll help you understand more about what God is doing in your life. When you finish that one . . . then I'll send you another."

"Thank you, sir." He bowed his head, a tear wrestling to

escape from his dimmed eyes. "Sir, I want most of all that you should pray for me and my people. My people are hungry for God's truth, and it is our responsibility to tell them."

I knelt down, hugging him tightly. "Innocent . . . I believe that God is going to use you to tell your people about His love. I'll help every way I can by long distance . . . but you've got to involve yourself in His church and life right here." I stretched myself, holding him at arm's length so that our eyes could meet. "Please know that someone cares and is praying for you in America," I whispered. He nodded his understanding, and without further words we parted.

Since that time I've heard from Innocent often. He has completed the Survival Kit Discipleship Training that I sent him, and he is deeply involved in a local church. He is also sharing his personal faith, and moving toward what he believes to be God's calling in his life.

A recent letter reads —

Dear Rev. Freeman:

I am glad to have this opportunity of writing you this letter at this precious time. By the amazing grace of God, I hope you are doing fine together with your family. I am quite alright with all members of my family, for God is caring for us in our daily life.

I have completed the Survival Kit which you sent. I am thanking you for sending this book. It has helped me learn more about Christianity and the Word of God. I am trusting the Lord, wishing to serve Him, and am daily telling others about Jesus. God's hand is upon me, and I am trying to be faithful.

I wish to send greetings to your church.

To the Laveen Baptist Church —

I am sending my warm Christian greetings to the people of Laveen Baptist Church. I have heard from Rev. Freeman that you are praying for me, and for this I am grateful. I am pleading with you to continue! If God allows, we will meet in Heaven, where we will sing, shout and pray for we shall have everlasting life. Pray for me as God prepares me to take His message to my country.

May our Lord Jesus Christ bless you all and guide you wherever you are.

From your friend,

Innocent Farai Mkansawire
Blantyre, Malawi
Central Africa

Two

Jimmy Hodges
Birth of a Vision

I

*H*eat.

It descended like a thick damp blanket across the Oklahoma City area, bringing in its wake the usual drainage of energies and flaring of tempers. It was always hot in July, but the summer of '84 seemed even more determined than usual to break the spirits of those who had chosen to make their home in the flat heartland of America.

People had raced to the would-be state years before, risking life and limb in a series of six "runs"; great throngs of people racing on horseback, in buggies and wagons, seeking to claim for themselves a small part of the 17 million acres of unassigned land that had been offered by the government. Some had jumped the gun, not waiting for the official start of the race, and these "Sooners" had ultimately given Oklahoma its nickname.

Some unsettled tracts had become cities in eight hours or less, and it was the city that was on Jimmy Hodge's mind on this particularly hot day. He and his wife Dee had been working out in the gym, and the ride home along the streets of Edmond had become increasingly hot and halting.

Turning the Mercury Linx onto Santa Fe Blvd., he spun the radio dial once again, vainly seeking some music that would soothe rather than unsettle.

"Thriller!"

It seemed as though every station in the city had ordered extra copies of the album, hell-bent on playing it between every string of droning commercials. Michael Jackson had won an unprecedented eight Grammys for the effort, and the sales of 37 million plus copies had evidently dictated that it fill the airwaves.

The stop at TCBY had provided a brief respite, but it was going to take more than yogurt to relieve the growing vertigo that was swallowing him. Suddenly, the dizziness dropped him into a darkness that he hadn't experienced before, and he collapsed over the steering wheel, sending the car into the left lane through honking traffic, finally to crash across a crude ditch and into an open field.

"Jimmy!"

Dee screamed it, reaching across the hot seat to shake his slumped form. Finally her cries and tears called him back into the immediate scene.

"I don't know what happened." He looked around, seemingly confused by his location. "I was just driving along, and then I just got so dizzy . . ."

"We've got to get you to the hospital," Dee cried.

He sat upright, taking several deep breaths. "I'm alright, now. It's just the heat or something. I'm not about to go to the hospital."

Hours later, after collapsing again at home, he found himself a patient at Mercy Hospital anyway.

"How long have you been aware that you have a heart irregularity?"

The doctor absentmindedly tapped his chin with his

pen, studying the chart before him during the interrogation.

"Well," Jimmy mused. "I've known since college days that I have some irregular heartbeats from time to time. It hasn't ever made me pass out or anything like that before."

"Technically," the doctor mumbled, "it's what we call Mitral Valve Prolapse Syndrome."

"Micro . . ." Jim felt Dee's hand squeeze his own, a shiver skittering up her thin arm.

"No," the doctor continued. "Not micro . . . Mitral. The Mitral valve is the value on the left side of the heart between the two chambers, the auricle and the ventricle. It's sorta . . . misfiring . . ."

Jim pushed himself back into the pillow, feeling drained and tired after the long days of being bedridden and tested. Needles stuck in his arms, hidden beneath white tape, tubes running from him to dripping bottles suspended on silver rods around his bed. Had he truly come all this way to die with a quivering heart?

"You're stabilized now," the doctor continued. "I think we can treat it with medication. There are some side effects that you should be aware of . . ."

"Like?" Jim had often been told that "the cure is worse than the disease," and he sensed that the doctor was preparing him for just such a disclosure.

"It'll slow you down. Slow down your body . . . it's supposed to do that. But, it'll probably also slow down your mental processes for awhile. There could be some bouts with real depression . . ."

"Do you have anything good to say?"

The doctor smiled. "It slows you down . . . but I think it'll keep you from quitting altogether." The promise of life had come packaged in a bundle of threat, and the doctor left them alone in the darkening room to contemplate their future.

Days later, Jim hoped that he was only having a classic mid-life crisis. The promised depression had come, and with it a great hurt that seemed to curl deep in the quick of his soul. It was, for him, a defining experience. A time to reevaluate a life lived and a ministry performed. What did God expect from him for the remainder of his days? Was he to continue with business as usual? Was he to use up his precious life following the same patterns that had marked his earlier years? Something deep within whispered that this couldn't be.

The initial seeds of this internal struggle had been planted in 1972 when he had made his first trip to the African country of Uganda to minister with missionary Webb Carroll. Uganda had suffered a long string of horrible tragedies since winning independence in 1962. Before that time, the country that Winston Churchill had called, "Pearl of Africa," had been prosperous and harmonious. However, the rise of brutal dictator Idi Amin quickly changed all of that. By the time of his overthrow in 1979, the country had been raped and squandered, a mere shadow of the beautiful land that Jim had experienced in his pilgrimage there. That first glimpse of the Dark Continent, coupled with other trips to Kenya in 1977 and 1984, had shown him a world where God was speaking and people were listening and responding by the thousands. He knew that God is always speaking everywhere, calling people to Himself. But, in Africa, he had experienced the broken heart of a people, and had watched them surrender themselves without reservation to God's love and grace.

Jim had felt that he had accomplished more there in weeks than he had in all of the rest of his ministry. This thought was magnified with the recent reminder that life is short at best, and that the Bible had been right when it had admonished all to "redeem the time."

It seemed so impossible somehow.

Such endeavors as full-time evangelism and concert ministries had proven to be demanding financially, and the idea of moving into a ministry that would demand such great financial cost and seemingly give back nothing in return seemed beyond his wildest dreams.

He had never tried to raise money, and didn't want to. The entire idea went against his grain, and he, like so many other men involved in similar ministries, simply wanted to use his gifts for God's glory in the widest possible arena without having to mess with demanding finances.

Yet, God had given him a vision of a new and distinctive type of mission. A ministry that would help to prepare Africans to reach Africans; a ministry that would make it possible to follow up and disciple the thousands who were responding to God's love. That vision, along with the deep call from somewhere within himself, pushed him forward into what he knew would ultimately be a life-changing decision.

"You're always here for me," he smiled. Dee sat across the table from him, her arms stretched forward so that she could clasp his hands. Although concerned about his health, she knew that there were some things even more important. She knew that a healthy body alone wouldn't release him from the calling that he was being confronted with. She was also well aware of his misgivings.

"I can't make finances a determining factor in this," he smiled. "I can't sift God's call and will through what I think I can do. I have to lift up my eyes and catch a glimpse of what God can do."

She nodded, smilingly lending approval.

"I know this," he whispered. "If this is to become a reality . . . God will have to provide. We can't do it . . . He'll have to." He paused, carefully choosing each word. "He'll have to do it . . . and when He does . . . we'll make sure that He gets all of the glory!"

That, Dee thought, sounded like a true recipe for success.

II

Jimmy Hodges had begun his life on October 3, 1937 in the bedroom of a simple farmhouse setting two miles east of Temple, Oklahoma. His father, Joseph, was a pipe line worker, always spending long hours welding on the web of oil and gas pipelines that dissected the area. The work demanded many moves, and he along with wife Billie Jo and son Jimmy, moved more than their share. One stop in Duncan had yielded brother D'Arcy when Jim was three.

"We must move everytime the rent comes due," Jim had often thought as a boy. From Oklahoma, to New Mexico, to Texas, and back to Oklahoma again. He once attended five schools in one year and seldom had opportunity to make friendships. He did, however, have his brother, and they spent the long summer days flooding tarantulas from their lairs, shooting frogs with rifle and slingshot, and busying themselves getting into every possible kind of childhood mischief.

It wasn't until the move to Velma, Oklahoma in 1950 that the family began to slow down and settle into a more rooted lifestyle. Located 18 miles east of Duncan, the small town of 600 plus people proved to be a welcome respite for a sixth grader who was tired of packing and unpacking.

The dry, rolling terrain was dotted with oil wells, giving his father ample work as a pumper and guager. A hard working, barrel-chested man, his father also fought his own personal demons. A long-time alcoholic, he often squandered his wages on binges, sometimes not coming home for days. Normally a gentle man, he became increasingly violent when in the grip of alcohol. Later, as a teenager, it would become Jim's responsibility to go into the bars, seeking his father, whom he would ultimately load into a car and drive home.

Always haunting the pool balls and card tables, his father was more than ready for a fight, even if it pitted him against a foe much larger than his 5'10" frame. One night Jim watched a large opponent charge his father, intent on taking his life. An agile swift kick to the chin sent the man flying against a wall, and sent the remaining coven of would-be attackers into retreat.

Even though his mother was an inactive Christian, Jim and D'arcy had never attended church before their move to Velma. One day a Sunday School teacher from First Baptist Church came to the small two room house sitting on the edge of the creek. The boys, having tired of catching crawdads, had been the ultimate center of the man's kindly invitation to attend.

"You'll like it, boys." The friendly man smiled, wiping his broad brow with a damp handkerchief. "We learn about a lot of exciting things that have taken place in this old world. Boys facing down giants with slingshots and faithful men standing up for something that really matters."

Jim and D'Arcy watched him warily, unsure of his intentions. They had never heard anyone speak of such things. They had heard about the fighting in Korea on the radio, and their father was forever grumbling beneath his breath about President Truman and the "crooks" in Washington. No one had mentioned anything about giants and people of faith who serve God. A tiny seed was planted, and although they didn't leave their childhood play to rush to the church house, they did remember the offer and pondered exactly what a Sunday School was supposed to be.

The First Baptist Church of Velma was a small wooden building, topped with a thin steeple that seemed, in Jimmy's vivid imagination, to scrape the basement of Heaven itself. The pastor was Dr. J.C. Bunn, a former Math teacher from South Carolina. He had left that profession, attended seminary, and had come to Velma as a first pastorate.

He was a tall man in his early 30's, well dressed, warm eyes dancing behind thin-rimmed glasses. He was driven by his love for the souls of people, and sometimes even stepped from the platform, standing on the front pew, pleading with individuals to step forward and give their lives to Jesus Christ. It was this man who ultimately brought Jim and D'Arcy to church. They had a sense that the pastor truly cared for them, and were also aware that First Baptist was definitely "the only show in town."

At the age of 13 Jim first became convicted of the fact that he was a sinner and that he truly needed a Saviour. For over two weeks a great spiritual war waged within him, until finally he could take it no longer. Stationed on the back row with brother D'Arcy, he once again heard the simple Gospel proclaimed and the Spirit of God wooed him until he felt that his young heart would burst within his chest.

The preacher paced back and forth on the small platform, his voice seemingly swirled by the waving handheld fans that dotted the small auditorium. It seemed to Jim that every word was directed toward him, and that every glance brought him eye to eye with the proclaimer of God's truth.

"We've been hearing a lot about North Korea's invasion of the south these days," the pastor whispered from behind the dark carved pulpit. "It looks like McArthur and the UN forces have their work cut out for them. But, I'm not talking about a hostile invasion this morning."

He moved forward, positioning himself squarely in the sunlight flowing through the large stained window nearby.

"I'm talking about a friendly invasion! I'm talking about the God Who created everything . . . stepping down to earth in the form of a man to walk in the midst of His own creation. I'm talking about how God loves YOU!!!" The personal pronoun bounced against Jim's tender heart. "I'm talking about how He sent His Son to pay the price for YOUR sins! I'm talking about being forgiven . . . I'm talking about becoming a part of God's family . . . I'm talking about living forever!"

As the final strains of the Invitation hymn were being sung, Jim walked down the aisle and prayed with the pastor, repenting of his sins and gladly inviting Jesus to come and dwell within him. Upon turning around, he found that his younger brother had followed him down the aisle, evidently intent on making the same life-changing decision for himself.

"What are you doing? Why did you follow me down here?" Jim whispered to his brother impatiently. The boy only smiled. "I didn't follow you. I followed Jesus," he said. "I guess we'll both just be following Him ... together ... from now on."

After they went home and shared their decision with their parents, their mother rededicated her life to Christ and she began to attend church with them. Both parents came to see their boys baptized one hot Sunday night, giving evidence through that ordinance of the reality that now lived within them.

"Now that we've said it, we need to live it." Jim wrapped his arm around D'Arcy's shoulders, pulling him close. "It can't just be words . . ."

D'Arcy smiled. He was thankful for his big brother's affirmation, and knew that the future would be somehow different than what they had experienced before.

Sometime later his father made a profession of faith during a Revival meeting, but even after this decision, he continued to fight a never-ending battle with alcohol that would plague him until his death.

He would occasionally withdraw into some secret place, seemingly trying to gather up enough strength to stand against his army of personal demons. It would work for awhile, and those times were islands of peace and relief for the family. Sooner or later, however, he'd fall again, returning home late at night, breaking furniture and sometimes flaying against unseen foes that sought his destruction.

During this time they moved 7 miles north of Velma, out on the baseline. Taking care of cattle in exchange for rent, the boys would faithfully hitchhike to church each Sunday or drive the old Federal Welding Truck, just a few years before they would be granted a legal Driver's License.

These days were carefully divided into compartments. Hours of hard work would be interspersed with time at church and dreamy days laying in the Johnson Grass, watching the thick, rich clouds rolling overhead and dreaming of places and people yet to be seen and experienced.

At the age of 14 some anonymous benefactor gave money so that Jim could attend the Southern Baptist Encampment at Falls Creek. It was in these surroundings, the hot air being swirled by whirring overhead fans in the great open air Tabernacle, that God spoke to his young heart once again. This time, not calling him to eternal life. Now, it was a quiet call to lay his new life down, so that he could give himself to God's ministry. The only ministry he knew anything about was being a "preacher," and so he surrendered to that call, expecting that God would give clearer direction as he moved forward day by day.

The world of music was opening wide to both Jimmy and D'Arcy at this time, and they were soon discovering a wide range of talents in that field. Jim became an accomplished drummer (he would ultimately win honors in Oklahoma State Drum competition) and began to play the Baritone horn. D'Arcy, for his part, began playing the cornet and they both began singing in church and in the school choir.

"D'Arcy, I want to give my talents back to the Lord," Jim shared late one evening. They had been sitting on the porch, captivated by their thoughts and only occasionally verbalizing what they were feeling. Always close, they knew each other well, and seldom needed to give prolonged explanations to one another.

"I know what you mean," D'Arcy answered. "There's more than enough people in the world using their voices for themselves."

"I guess we march to the beat of a different drummer," Jim laughed. "The Lord gave me a song, and I want to sing it for Him. The Book of Revelation says that all things were created for His pleasure, and I think He means for me to bring pleasure to people . . . and Him . . . through my music."

It didn't need to be said. Both had known that they would ultimately give their all for God and His Kingdom. No, it didn't need to be said . . . but both were glad that they had said it anyway.

By the time Jim entered the Ninth Grade, he was beginning to accept invitations to lead music in Revival meetings for country churches around the state. Another trip to Falls Creek helped him clarify his calling not only to preach, but to the ministry of the Gospel through music.

"Here I am, Lord!" He cried it . . . and he meant it. He was ready to sing God's praises, and hopefully, could help to lead many others into the joyous reality he had discovered for himself.

When Jim began his Sophomore year of high school, they once again moved to the town of Duncan. Once a cattle town on the old Chisholm Trail, it had become a center for both oil exploration and agriculture. There, at Immanuel Baptist Church, he got his first true taste of evangelism. Evangelist Freddie Gage came to preach a crusade in the church, and many young people came to Christ during the week of special services. As Jim watched the life-changing pageant, he began to see even more clearly the real potential of proclaiming the Gospel and seeing many respond to God's call.

He intensified his attempt to accept invitations to do music for revivals throughout the area, and often wondered at God's powerful moving through his widening musical gifts.

Months later his parents separated, and Jim, along with his mother and D'Arcy, moved from Duncan to live briefly on the flat, wind-blown plain that was called Tatum, New Mexico.

Moving back to Duncan once again for his final year of high school, Jim threw himself headlong into both school life and his search for involvement in God's ministry. He was voted "Most Talented" in his class, started a Teen Morning Watch which allowed many of the young people to gather together daily for a brief devotional time, and was taken onto the staff at Immanuel Baptist Church as Youth Director and Assistant Music Director.

It was in the preaching and singing at the Rescue Mission and work in Revivals, however, that he found his greatest satisfaction. He stood before congregations, both large and small, lifting his clear powerful voice in worship and celebration. As the music filled the chamber, he often looked into the eyes of the people gathered there. Although he was singing to His Lord, he became acutely aware that the music was touching hearts, often ministering to deep spiritual needs and drawing people toward a Saviour and His precious promises. It seemed that he was truly "on course," and he longed for the day that he could break all restraints, both real and imagined, and move ever forward into God's service.

"I don't think I can keep up with it anymore." He leaned against the bare table separating him from his friend, seemingly relieved that he was able to drop the facade he had been carrying through recent weeks.

"My folks are finally getting a divorce, and it's the straw breaking my back. Forget the camel!"

His first year at Oklahoma Baptist University had been draining. His studies, coupled with his church responsibilities and family hurts, had woven together to drive his grades steadily downward.

"I don't have the money to stay around here." He was glad to hear himself say it at last. The only way he had been able to come in the first place was through a Drum Scholarship.

Everyone had been impressed with his demonstration on the snare drum, accidentally breaking the tip off the stick early in the program and continuing on to victory. He knew his drums, and they had "beaten" him into the realm of further education. Now, however, he felt more beaten than they. He was drained, heartsick, discouraged and plain old tired of it all.

His friend dropped his head, unable to say anything that would offer much solace.

"I'm thinking about joining the service," Jim continued. "I went up to Fort Sill and auditioned for the Naval Academy of Music. I've been accepted. All I need is my physical, taking the oath, and heading for Boot Camp."

He bowed his head, silently examining his hands. It was a route far removed from what he had envisioned. But, at least, it might release him from the current situation so that he could regroup and determine what was best.

That night, alone in the darkness, he knelt against the platform at the front of the church auditorium. He had been praying for hours, begging God for some direction. The moon glowed through the stained glass windows, casting an array of errant shadows across the floor. It seemed as though a parade of possibilities were projected there; glimpses of people and places yet unknown and unexplored. He realized that this was truly a "crossroads decision." He would determine a course of action that would likely set his direction for years to come. Now, more than ever, he needed insight beyond his own.

Finally, he poked into his pocket. Finding a single coin, he threw it into the air.

"Lord, show me," he whispered. "Heads I stay . . . tails I go."

Although he hadn't read of a similar decision making process in the Bible, he accepted the luck of the draw. He resigned his position at the church and began the process of entering the Armed Services of his country.

Days later he was laying stripped on a cold examination table, an Air Force doctor listening inquisitively to his chest. The physician grunted, disappeared and then brought others in to listen.

Jim shrugged nervously, slowly beginning to feel like a laboratory specimen in a high school classroom back in Duncan.

"It's a classic textbook Mitral Valve Prolapse sound," the doctor muttered. "We don't get a chance to hear one too often."

"Glad I could make your day," Jim thought. He hadn't

heard of a Mitral Valve before, but it didn't sound like something that you would want to have anything happen to.

He was later informed that he had passed the physical, and was given two weeks to clear up his affairs so that he could take the bus to Colorado Springs for Boot Camp.

He wouldn't make it.

His father suffered a massive heart attack the following week in Duncan and he got a postponement. Waiting through the Summer, he ultimately made his way back to OBU to say "good-bye" to his friends.

A late night prayer meeting with them didn't clarify his situation. "I need you guys to pray with me, " he implored. "I just can't seem to get a handle on what I'm supposed to do. I thought it was all settled, and then my dad's heart attack seemed to slow the process."

His friends gathered around him, hands outstretched to rest upon his head and shoulders, seeking to both encourage and remind him of their friendship and earnest prayers.

"Lord, I want to do what's right. The fight to stay in school has been overwhelming, and it's drained every ounce of strength that I have. I want to use my talents, but I just don't see a way. If there is one . . . show me."

As he drove through the night back toward Duncan, he became increasingly convinced that the move toward the military was outside God's will for his life. The following day was the last opportunity to enroll in college, and he knew that he had no money. He would even have to borrow gas money to get him there if he chose to return to school. He, however, couldn't shake the ever present conviction that it was the Lord's will for this particular moment that he complete his education.

"He'll make a way," Jim mumbled beneath his breath, pressing his car filled with his few earthly belongings toward the campus. "If He doesn't . . . then I'll fall on my face right here and now. But . . . I know that He's going to make a way!"

He enrolled for classes on the last day and was immediately called by a church in Lawton to serve as their Minister of Music and Education . . . and "Associate" to the Janitor. They were willing to pay him $20.00 per week to drive back and forth between there and school. During those days he watched as the attendance of the church grew from 100 to over 650 under the leadership of Pastor J. Harold Bryan. Bryan had a hot heart for souls, and used many "full-time" evangelists to help in the reaping ministry of the church. Jim had never seen God bless and work in such a way, and those days were a true source of encouragement.

"I'm glad that the decisions of my life aren't left to the casting of lots and the whims of mindless fate," he chuckled to himself. "I don't know what the future holds . . . but I know that God holds my hand and He'll lead me one step at a time if I'll let him."

In February of 1962, Jimmy resigned his position in Lawton and entered a ministry of full-time evangelism. Often working with brother D'Arcy, they alternately preached and sang, lifting up Jesus through the proclamation of God's rich promise. In church buildings and football stadiums Jim watched as God used his talent to translate the Gospel. He averaged 42 crusades per year for the next five years.

IV

He was 27 years old when he went to lead the Crusade at Webster Avenue Baptist Church in Lakeland, Florida. Pastor Ernie Habecker introduced him to a cute young widow with two children who was an active part of his fellowship. After the Crusade concluded they began to correspond. Between letters Jim spent a major part of his income making telephone calls, carrying on a long distance "courting" process with the dark, beautiful young lady.

It surprised no one when he accepted an Interim position at Lakeland during his "off season" of November, December and January. He claimed that it was to escape the ice and snow, but most believed that his intentions went far beyond the local weather.

He married his beloved Dee the following June, and then adopted Robin and Steven. Two years later their daughter Shelli joined them as the youngest member of the Hodges clan.

The ministry of evangelism was expectedly demanding. He would sometimes be gone between 280 and 300 days each year, returning to their home in Lakeland whenever possible to recharge his batteries and prepare for another long haul down the road. Dee and the children traveled with him during the summer months as much as possible, often adding their diverse talents to the work of the ministry.

In 1969, Jim met Webb Carroll, Missionary to the African nation of Uganda. The missionary challenged Jim repeatedly, seeking to lay the burden of his people squarely on the young man's mind.

"Don't a lot of evangelists come to Africa?" He couldn't imagine such a rich spiritual harvest going for years without laborers.

"No," Webb frowned. "Not too many come our way. We have so many people who are hungry for the Gospel. Missionaries have been planting precious seed for years, but they are so totally outnumbered."

Jim leaned back, trying to visualize masses of people seeking after God's love and truth. Surely this was a logical place for an evangelist to be. He purposed in his heart that he would put together an evangelistic team to minister in that arena. Three years later that plan became a reality.

In 1972, several things happened in our world. President Nixon visited both China and Russia, Gov. George Wallace, while running for the presidency, was shot by Arthur Bremer and partially paralyzed. Apollo Astronauts John Watts and Charles Duke spent 71 hours on the surface of the moon, Jackie Robinson, the first black man to play major league baseball died, and Jimmy Hodges first planted his feet on the hardened clay of the "Dark Continent."

The 19 man team traveled to Jinja, Uganda. The community lay on the shores of Lake Victoria, the headwaters to the Nile. Although it was a major marketing center for southern Uganda, it still had a "small town" feel that belied its importance to the region. The 19 man team, once settled, spread out in all directions. Jim, along with longtime friend Wayne Bristow, spent three long weeks living in a tent, working with the dynamic African preacher Arthur Kinyanjui.

As a young man, Kinyanjui had been gripped by the Gospel of Christ. Quickly surrendering to the ministry, he was soon preaching everywhere, starting churches and calling his own people to repentance and new life.

Taking his 7 children with him, he then began a work with the Karamajung tribe for several years. These giant people, whose men were usually at least 7 feet tall, were known for their primitive lifestyle and the way they always went naked. This ministry reaped great result, and his faithful labors there, along with extended preaching tours in other areas, won him a rich reputation.

Later, during the Mau Mau uprising that would ultimately lead to Kenya's independence, both sides wanted him to lend his support. He refused.

"I will stand in the middle and preach the Gospel to all!" This bold stand was honored by God and man alike. Later, the new Kenyatta Government of Kenya recognized him as a leader with great spiritual credibility, and his opportunities to minister grew endlessly from that moment on. He had total access to both the common people and those in high government position. To all he offered the same refrain . . . "New life in Jesus Christ!"

Jim entered into a 10 year team relationship with Evangelists Wayne Bristow and Felix Snipes. This three man team was used mightily of the Lord to preach the Gospel across the nation and around the world. Football stadiums and churches across America were filled nightly with people in search for lasting answers. In December of 1980, without warning, Jim's brother D'Arcy went home to be with the Lord that he had served so faithfully.

This loss, coupled with the breakup of the team in the Spring of 1981, threw Jim into what he suspected was a classic mid-life crisis. He sat down to evaluate his options, and found them all to be strangely unexciting. He could go back into church evangelism alone, work on the widening of his concert ministry, or give more attention to overseas endeavors.

A great sense of futility swept over him. He sat in the shadows, alternately praying and weeping. The death of his brother had vividly reminded him of the brevity of life. If D'Arcy, seemingly in good health, could be swept away . . .

He knew more than anything else that he wanted to count as much as possible during his remaining time. "It doesn't matter whether I have five more minutes or fifty more years," he whispered. "I want it to count! I want to make a difference! I want to know that I've lived my life in the center of Your will, Lord!" His prayers seemed to bounce from the ceiling, returning to ring in his own ears. "I want to know that the gifts and abilities that you've given me have been well invested. I just want to count . . . or . . . oh, Lord! Please! Either excite my heart with a great sense of direction — or take me home to be with You!"

It was a cry that erupted from his great depression. A desire to reach a maximum number of people for Christ in the shortest amount of time coupled with a deadening sense of futility concerning the future. He pressed forward into the christian concert arena, watching God bless his concert and recording ministry. It was, however, on the other side of the world that he would ultimately find the answers and sense of purpose that his heart cried for.

Arthur Kinyanjui, then pastoring the Nakuru Baptist Church in Kenya, invited Jim to come and minister in his field of labor. Greeting his friend at Nairobi Airport, Arthur hurriedly loaded the equipment and luggage into the back of his battered car and began the long drive through the congested streets of the city.

"Bwana," he sighed. "There are many Christians here. They are so much in need of teaching and training. They are like Jesus saw them. They are like sheep without a shepherd."

"What about the pastors?"

"We have many good men, but most of them are doing a poor job. They don't really know how to minister to their people. They don't even know how to build themselves in their own faith and relationship with their Lord."

Jim watched the masses parading past the dirty windshield. It was impossible to imagine. A land where God was working, and yet so few who could minister to them. "Why haven't they been trained? Aren't there any seminaries?"

Arthur smiled. "Oh yes, Bwana. We have some good schools. But most of the men who pastor in these areas can't afford schooling. Most have large families . . . eight or nine children and a wife . . . and they make less than $30.00 a month . . . if they are well paid."

They rode silently for a long time. The Spirit of the Lord was revising and mingling the facts with a great burden that had been born in his heart years before when he had set foot on the Dark Continent for the first time. Somehow, deep within himself, he had suspected all along that his destiny and Godly purpose was linked with the people of Africa . . . and beyond that . . . a lost and dying world.

Jim looked into the haunted eyes of the people they passed. They moved past his vantage point like a snaking parade. Willowy women, bundles of wood and cracked pottery precariously balanced on their heads; weathered men, their bare feet hardened by their forced marches back and forth across the usually hostile land; children sitting along the broken roadside, their eyes vacant, almost blind to the world that seemed to methodically pass them by. All of the drama of life and death being played out in a continent that had suffered painfully beneath the heavy weight of war, famine and disease.

He remembered the words of Lucretius, taught to him in some almost forgotten classroom. *"The wailing of the new-born infant is mingled with the dirge for the dead."* Were these not the people for whom Christ had died? Were they not the masses to which the church had been sent? Was this not the time to touch them with God's love and precious Gospel?

"Let me ask you something, Arthur." Jim shifted in the seat, focusing his total attention on his host. "What if the Lord were able to pull together a ministry that could give training to these pastors? What if we were able to bring a teaching staff from the states, invite pastors to attend a training conference with their expenses paid, and then take those men out into the market places and villages for some "hands on" training in preaching crusades, sharing their faith, and discipling believers?"

"Is such a thing possible?" Arthur's eyes grew bigger as he considered the possibilities.

"Only in the mind of God," Jim said. "He would have to do it. He'd have to give the direction and provide the means. But I believe that He is planning to move on your land like no one has ever imagined before. I believe that He might be willing to use us to do such a thing . . .if we're willing to trust

Him and give Him all the honor and glory for the miracles that we're going to see!"

It began slowly. An initial Conference and Crusades in Kenya's capital city of Nairobi in 1986 was followed by a flood of life-changing projects. Mombasa, Kenya . . . Tukuyu, Tanzania . . . Kisumu, Kenya . . . Embu, Kenya . . . Moshi and Arusha in Tanzania . . . Bukoba, Tanzania . . . Mwanza, Tanzania . . . Dar es Salaam, Tanzania . . . Kigoma, Tanzania . . . Dodoma, Tanzania . . . Lilongwe, Bujumbura, Burundi and Blantyre, Malawi. The list went on and on. Hundreds of pastors trained and inflamed, involving themselves in classes that prepared them for ministry coupled with crusade services that gave ample opportunity to practice what they had learned. Thousands upon thousands of people stepping forward to embrace Jesus as Lord of their lives. The starting of countless new missions, churches and preaching points, now manned by men who were better able to minister to their people and lead the congregations forward in reaching their own people for Christ.

During these days of ministry the Lord continued to gather a company of dedicated men and women in America. They caught the vision that God had given, and invested their unique talents and abilities into the widening work around the world. A dedicated and Godly Board of Directors was assembled that lent leadership and great credibility to the ministry.

Ben Manis had been a teenager in Jim's Youth Group in Lawton, Oklahoma. After a separation of 20 years, the Lord drew them back together with a common purpose. Now a successful businessman, Manis set aside his business pursuits and gave himself totally to the ministry. Launching out ahead of all others, he moves year after year into untouched corners of the world, preparing the fields for the upcoming Conferences and Crusades. His love of Jesus, business acumen and adventurous spirit serves him well as he labors tirelessly for a lost and dying world.

"The secret of winning Africa for Christ is simple," Jim had often mused. "We must help Africans to reach Africans." That great dream took another giant step forward when the first Chichewa language All National Project was held in Mzuzu, Malawi. The Hodges organization provided funding, materials, equipment and personnel from the states to help organize the effort. All of the teaching and preaching, however, was done entirely by Africans who had been carefully trained and prepared in previous projects.

A total of 88 pastors were trained in this unique project, and in the week of crusades following the Training Institute almost 17,000 people gave their hearts and lives to Christ. This great move of God's Spirit was reflected in the life of the Mzuzu Baptist Church. Running an average of 50 people on Sunday morning before the Conference and Crusades, they were greeted with a crowd of 723 on their first Sunday following the event. 512 of these were new converts who were coming for baptism and discipling. Another 103 people, friends who came to church at the invitation of the new Christians, made their decision for Christ during that Morning Worship Service.

The effects of the Mzuzu Project were far reaching. Many key leaders in the villages and communities . . . chiefs and teachers . . . were born into God's Kingdom. Nine new churches were established immediately following the event, and more people are coming to Christ with the passing of each new day.

Both Swahili and Chichewa speaking crusade teams have now been trained and they are pushing deeper into the African continent each week, preaching the Gospel in villages, market places and schools. The Hodges Ministry also continues to provide bicycles for pastors who lead several congregations, allowing them to traverse the great distances between preaching points with greater ease and speed.

"The Lord has put together a unique ministry," Jim shares at every given opportunity. "It's built on the ministries of strongly gifted men and women here in the states. The Lord prepares them, and then blends them together during these projects so that they can be positioned to see their gifts and ministries maximized. Of course," he quickly adds, "it's the Lord alone who ultimately touches the hearts of the masses, and we give Him all honor and glory for the great things He has allowed us to be a part of!"

Now doors of opportunity open in every direction. More African nations are ready for the touch of God's hand, and exciting possibilities are surfacing in India and Europe. "The vision translates to all cultures and lands," Jim smiles. "Teach people to reach their own people. Train them and then take them out into the fields and show them that it all really works! Let them watch God move in the hearts of the people, and then try to stop them! Our wildest imagination can't begin to grasp all that the Lord is preparing to do around the world during these exciting days!"

And the things you have heard me say in the presence of many witnesses entrust to reliable men who will also be qualified to teach others.

—II Timothy 2:2 NIV

Three

True Tales of Africa

"Behold What God Hath Done . . ."

The Valley of Death

*I*saac only escaped his world once. Pushing beyond the pitted encircling streets that formed the crude barrier around his own land, he ran through smoke-belching buses and honking traffic, finally straying down a narrow sidewalk that led to the heart of Kenya's capital of Nairobi.

He picked his way through the maze of street merchants, their treasures spread on stained mats; past the dark shuttered shops mostly owned by merchants from India, their wares carefully displayed behind dust-enshrouded glass.

Finally, he stood on Mama Ngina Street, near the intersection of Moi Avenue. Positioning himself amidst a cluster of crippled beggars, he swept his eyes upward, trying to catch a glimpse of the rooftop swimming pool that supposedly crowned the Hilton Hotel.

It was true! Other boys had made the pilgrimage before him, returning with fantastic stories of buildings that gleamed like the sun and stretched upward to scrape the clouds from the sky. They had told of the white tables, protected by delicate umbrellas, that surrounded the Intercontinental Hotel. They had drooled as they recounted the aromas wafting from the Thorn Tree Cafe, nestled in the shadow of the New Stanley Hotel. But nothing in the reports had captured his imagination like the rooftop swimming pool.

He shaded his eyes with a dirty hand, squinting vainly to catch a glimpse of some slender form preparing to dive into the promised cool water.

"Get away from here, boy!" A beggar swatted at him, angered by his presence. "You don't belong here! People can't walk through you! Get away!"

Isaac slid into the shadows, edging around the marble facade of the monolithic structure. His eyes danced across the dainty merchandise nestled on velvet in the shop windows. Necklaces and bracelets; carvings and crystal shaped like animals that he had only heard of. A weaving of voices and dialects filled the cold air flowing through the huge glass doors. Beyond, in the darkness, he could barely see people gathered around a smooth carved table, huddling over paperwork, surrounded by ringing telephones and whirling fans.

"What are you doing here?" The strong gloved hand locked to his shoulder was connected to a dark towering figure, carefully adorned in a red uniform, outlined with silver braids and flowing tassels.

"We don't need any street scum cluttering up the doorway," he growled beneath his breath. "Wherever you came from," he paused, giving added threat to his words, "I suggest you run back there!"

Isaac needed no further instructions. He bolted down the street, ripping through braying beggars and startled pedestrians. Past the stately banks of the world, through the tangled traffic, breathlessly pressing toward the invisible boundaries of his own domain.

Isaac's home, although only minutes from the Hilton Hotel, was a dark, primitive world called the Mathare Valley. An ugly gash carved in the dusty terrain, it was filled with crude abodes fashioned from rusting metal, rotting wood and pungent clots of mud and clay.

Refugees from other parts of the continent had gathered there, seeking to escape political oppression and starving droughts. The lines of demarcation within his world came in the form of crooked narrow alleys, meandering through the smoke-filled hovels. Crowds of people wandered aimlessly through these corridors, most seemingly having no place to go. Children sat beside the open sewers, laughing and making mud pies out of the stinking slime that oozed along the thoroughfares.

Isaac's family had been, in some ways, lucky. Most of the tattered dwellings housed three or four families, huddled together in hot, stinking surroundings smaller than the cheapest room at the Hilton Hotel. They, however, had been able to build their own one room dwelling, his father ingeniously fashioning it out of discarded materials he had found across the sprawling city that surrounded them.

"We live in filth, but we don't have to be filthy." His father had said it a thousand times, seeking to teach as he passed the meager portions of ugali and beans to Isaac and his two sisters. "We live on a dirt floor, but your mother sweeps it many times each day." Isaac could almost hear his mother's smile. "We don't have much to eat, but we do eat. I find the work that I can, and we'll have more someday."

Isaac was proud of his father. His courage had led them away from the starvation of their own land, and even though the promises of Kenya had not yet been experienced, they had been able to maintain some form of dignity and family structure.

"Where you lead me, I will go." His mother had uttered it upon their departure, and they had all kept their word.

Now, they had added the refrain, "What you feed me, I will eat."

A hot brilliant sun was beating down on the valley the day the wazungu first came. Isaac had seen them occasionally during his twelve years, most often skittering around the edges of his world. Usually dressed in strange clothing, neatly pressed and topped with wide-brimmed hats, they looked to him like faded phantoms, pink and pale like the dying light of the harvest moon on the fields of his former home.

This particular band of white people had been wandering through the Valley for days, finally focusing an a broad field that stretched in the heart of the tightly gathered structures. They had then busied themselves, clearing away the decaying animal carcasses, sweeping the human and animal waste toward the perimeter, and shooing the meandering goats away from the heart of the dusty lot.

Isaac lingered near the leader of the group, listening to him talk, subtly perfecting his broken English. He would never run to the white stranger like the younger children. They delighted in the hair on the man's pale arms, and laughed and giggled as they gathered around and tentatively rubbed his reddening skin.

He, rather, hung back with the older boys, wary and uncertain of the stranger's intentions. What would cause such a man to come from the other side of the world to clear a field in the decaying valley? Such actions demanded caution and distrust from anyone who was old enough to consider them.

Soon a van arrived, followed by a pickup, and finally a bus pulled in, filled with African men, dressed in frayed suits, their hands filled with black books and boxes overflowing with other supplies.

"What do they want here?" Isaac asked the question of his friend Benson standing nearby. His comrade frowned and shrugged. "My father says that the wazungu are all rich and crazy," he whispered. "The men in the bus must be their servants." He shivered. "I don't want to be one."

The back of the van was opened, revealing a wondrous array of equipment, covered with dials and gauges. A mzungu began to affix cords to the machinery, soon uncoiling them to attach to speakers that were being erected on both sides of a platform that had been moved into the heart of the area. Uncoiling a long orange cord, another man began to climb over the neighboring rooftops, apparently looking for some source of electricity that could be used to breathe life into the cold dead appliance.

Isaac laughed beneath his breath, mentally detailing the distance that would have to be traversed to find such a source. While this activity was underway, the men from the bus had begun to mill through the growing crowd, gathering small gaggles of people, sharing with them the booklets that they clutched in their hands. Isaac slipped forward, trying to hear.

They were speaking of Mungu and of His love for everyone. They were telling of a mzee named Jesus. Isaac had heard the name, but couldn't remember where. His father had been raised Islamic, and had sought to instill rich values into the lives of his children. The name Jesus had been mentioned by him and others in passing, but this Jesus seemed to be the central message of the men sharing amidst the crowd.

A moan from one of the speakers gave immediate evidence that a power source had been found, and Isaac pushed forward, drawn like a moth to flame. He perched just outside the perimeter of the ropes that had been strung around the platform. Music was playing now, dancing through the valley, drawing a growing flow of people into the circle. He listened intently, first to young African men singing, and then to the choir from the tiny church huddled at the end of an alley nearby.

Finally, the tall mzungu stepped onto the platform, an African man standing next to him. As he spoke, his companion beside him repeated his words again in Swahili, carefully shadowing his every move. "We have come from America to bring you good news," he cried. He smiled and lifted the black book in his hand toward the sky. "The God who created everything also created you! He loves you and I come bringing a message from Him!"

For twenty minutes Isaac stood huddled amidst the crowd, listening to the wondrous story. A God who created everyone with a desire to love them and have that love returned. Man's decision to go his own way, and the great gulf of sin that made spiritual life for man impossible without God's intervention. The sending of a Holy Son, the death at the hands of cruel men, and the step from the grave into life again. The promise that anyone could come to God through this Son and His sacrifice. The tale bore all of the elements of a reality seldom known in the valley; the story was built upon a foundation of true hope.

Having moved the younger children to another part of the field to hear the story again from special teachers, the man paused and extended a simple invitation.

"I believe that many here are being called by God to Himself. I believe that many want to turn and walk God's way. I believe that many want to invite this Jesus to come and dwell within them as Saviour and Lord. Today, I'm going to give you an opportunity to receive the gift of forgiveness and everlasting life."

He paused, bowed his head in silent prayer, and the ropes in front of Isaac were dropped, allowing people to step over and stand before the crude wooden platform. Isaac, uncertain of the decision that was being made by so many others, jumped back. He glanced at Benson, motioning to him from across the field. The flow of those receiving the message from God caught him for an instant, and then he broke free and moved to the sidelines.

"Look at all those who are going forward," Benson whispered. "I'm glad that I didn't stay and listen to all of the talk."

"You didn't hear?" Isaac had assumed that his friend had heard and rejected.

Benson nodded negatively. Isaac's heart sank. Benson was standing on the wayside out of ignorance. He, on the other hand, had heard and been stirred by the message. His decision to retreat seemed tragic somehow as he watched the crowd of people praying before him.

He went to his mat early that night. The room was hot, thick with the smell of cooking fires and human waste. Dogs barked endlessly in the distance, mingling their yowling cries with those of babies and the angry shouts of people cramped too closely together in the night. Pale moonlight washed through the open door, illuminating the fine dust that habitually danced in the air.

A strange calm had descended over the valley after a late afternoon disturbance. A thief had been caught by a crowd, stoned and ultimately burned to death. The police arrived much too late to do any more than gather up the raw, charred remains. There would be no arrests. It was an unspoken fact that anyone stupid or desperate enough to steal from those who have nothing could expect such a fate. No, there would be no investigation and no arrests concerning the incident.

His father sat outside, leaning against the rough walls, thoughtlessly drawing designs in the dust with a sharpened stick.

"Who are you stranger?"

His father's inquiry tugged Isaac from the outer borders of slumber where he had been loitering. He leaned upward, barely able to glimpse the man outlined in the flickering light outside. Short, slumped, his rumpled suit seemingly sizes too big for his narrow frame. His dusty shoes were bound together with thick strands of tape. His round jowled face housed dark dull eyes, set close together above a bulbous nose and thick cracked lips.

"My name is Stephen," he whispered. "I've been here sharing God's good news, and I have no place to sleep."

Isaac's father stood and extended his hand. "You can sleep on our floor," he said invitingly. "No one gets turned away from our home who bears good news."

Later that night, the stranger sat in the middle of the room, Isaac and his family gathered around him. He had told of the Pastor's Conference that he had attended at the Brackenhurst Baptist Conference Center in Limuru. Isaac remembered the area from their pilgrimage to Nairobi. A vast sea of coffee and tea plantations, blanketing rolling hills outlined by stately groves of conifer and eucalyptus trees.

"I'm originally from Uganda," he told them. "I served God even then, but when Idi Amin came into power he sought my life. Some missionaries smuggled me out of the country in a coffin. They drilled small holes so that I could breathe, and then they hauled me past the border guards into Kenya."

Isaac shivered, trying to imagine the confining darkness of such a journey.

"I'm almost blind," the stranger continued. "They had to lead me to my classes at the Conference. But . . ." His dull eyes brightened, ignited by a thought. "I'm glad that I came. I've never truly been able to tell others what I have experienced myself. This Conference taught me to share my faith . . . and I've been doing that."

"You were on the bus?" Isaac was, for the first time, aware that his father had known of the gathering on the dusty field earlier in the day.

"Yes," the stranger smiled. "They taught us to share our faith and then sent us out to do it while they prepared for the service. I was so busy doing it . . . I guess I lost track of time. I missed the bus . . ."

"Have many received your message?" Isaac was again surprised by his father's openness.

"Over one hundred have prayed with me today to receive Jesus as Lord." He dug deeply into his coat pocket, finally pulling a wad of paper into the dim light. "These are records of their decisions. They'll be receiving Bible Studies and help so that they can grow strong in their new life."

His father leaned back, stroking the knot of stubble cresting on his chin. "Why don't you tell us this good news," he said. "I heard part of it in the field earlier today, and I know that my son heard it too."

Isaac allowed his eyes to meet those of his father. A knowing smile flickered across his parent's face. "I think we all need to hear this news."

The morning sun brought a new day. The new day brought a new life for Isaac and his family. Through that long night the crumpled stranger had shared the promise of God's love and the availability of forgiveness and eternity. After the promises from the Holy Book had been carefully read, they had each bowed their head and stepped from the Mathare Valley into the suburbs of Heaven itself. The stranger hugged each of them, promising that others would come to help them better understand the life that they were now living.

Later that day Isaac drew his friend Benson aside into the shadows. "Benson," he smiled, "I've heard some news that has changed my life and . . ." He put his dark, callused hand on his friend's thin shoulder. "And, since you're my friend, I think that I need to share it with you . . ."

"Go ye therefore and make disciples . . ."

The Sacrifice Tree

*U*ntil the late 1800's there was nothing there but a swampy watering hole for the cattle of Masai tribesmen. The Mombasa to Uganda Railway, however, changed all of that. Soon the iron rails laid by indentured Indian laborers from Gujarat and Punjab brought an evergrowing stream of would-be adventurers, colonialists and farmers into the area.

Now, almost a century later, Nairobi had become the largest city between Cairo and Johannesburg. An island of pavement, glass and towering steel set in the heart of a flat plain still roamed by rhinos, giraffes and stalking lions and cheetahs.

Mark wiped his brow, reminding himself that it was supposedly Winter in Kenya. The hot equatorial sun beat down upon his shoulders, his tan shirt deflecting most of the heat to his rapidly reddening neck.

"I thought this hat would help," he said, pulling the brim of the crumpled chapeau more forcefully toward the bridge of his nose.

"It has," his translator encouraged. "You should have seen your bald spot before you started wearing it!" He flashed a now familiar smile, laughing inwardly at his joke. Daniel was enjoying every minute of working with the preachers who had come from America. He had been taught much during the Pastor's Conference, but nothing could replace this opportunity to learn witnessing and crusade techniques first-hand.

"Daniel, I was hoping that we could set up down there." Mark's finger directed his guide to the broad stretch of flat-tened abodes tucked lazily in the valley surrounding Lake Nairobi. "Are you sure we can't actually get down there where the people are?"

Daniel shook his head negatively. "No room, Bwana. The houses are too thick and close together. We'd never get the truck and van in. Even if we did . . . we wouldn't have room for any people to come and hear us."

"That would defeat the whole purpose of the thing," Mark mused. "What are our options?"

"You're standing in the middle of it."

Mark looked around at the barren hilltop, adorned with wilted grass and dotted with wandering goats. The site was exactly the opposite of everything he had schooled himself to look for.

"Flexibility," he muttered to himself. "When in Africa . . . remember the key word you're always throwing around to your team members. You MUST be flexible!"

Daniel waved his hand, inviting a nearby herdsman to join them. The two men conversed for a few moments in Swahili, waving their arms and pointing in every possible direction. Mark wondered if the conference was designed to simplify or aggravate the situation.

"Bwana, he says that if you set up here . . . some people will come."

"Where?"

"You can set up everything under that tree."

Mark's eyes followed his companion's gaze, settling on a lone tree standing at the edge of the slope that overlooked the village below. Its gnarled roots undulated above and below the hardened surface of the ground, obviously seeking every possible drop of precious water to feed the tangled web of branches that reached upward from the thick trunk.

"Not much shade there." Mark was embarrassed by the first thought that ran through his mind. It sounded like nothing was more important than getting into some protection from the boiling sun.

Mark waved to the drivers and soon the van and pickup were carefully positioned beneath the spreading branches. The sound system was activated, sending a rush of music across the valley, another team member blending with the chorus extending an invitation for people to join them there.

"Bwana . . . this is a special place," Daniel whispered. "The herdsman told me that this is the 'Sacrifice Tree'."

"Sacrifice . . . ?"

"The people here have offered sacrifices to their gods beneath this tree through the centuries. It's been a sacred place for many."

Mark watched as a handful of people emerged from the houses below, slowly working their way up the hillside toward them. Others could be seen peeking from their doorways, shading their eyes from the glaring sun, seeking the source of the music and invitation being extended from the summit.

Finally, a small knot of people assembled there, gathering tightly around the platform. Planted in the center of the group were five Masai warriors. Tall, regal, dressed in traditional flowing robes, these noble people had resisted all attempts to be drawn into the Twentieth Century. They had avidly disregarded the tide of change awash across the continent from the Western world.

Their infrequent contacts with "civilization" in the past had been less than enriching. They had suffered greatly from the British colonization. Rinderpest, an infectious disease evidently brought by the British to the African continent, had decimated their cattle herds, quickly bringing famine and smallpox. The weakened people had tried to fight back, but had been defeated and ultimately relocated in southern Kenya and Tanzania.

The Masai men are rigidly classed by age into boys, warriors, and elders. These men were obviously from the proud warrior ranks, and their very presence in the crowd was both surprising and strangely unnerving.

After the music had faded, Mark mounted the platform and searched the questioning eyes of the people standing before him. He swept his hand upward, outlining the tangled tentacles of wood that slightly shaded him from the sun.

"I've been told that this is called the 'Sacrifice Tree.' Your ancestors have come to this place through the years to make their offerings to their gods." A knowing look spread across the faces, seemingly surprised that he knew the history of the place.

"I've come here to to tell you of another 'sacrifice tree.' It wasn't a tree like this one. It wasn't a tree created by God to shade the weary worker and to provide fruit for hungry children. It was a tree built by man. It wasn't created for man's enrichment . . . it was created for man's destruction!" The group drew more tightly before the platform, somehow drawn to the message.

"The one true God created this tree and all trees! He placed the nighttime moon and sprinkled the heavens with a sea of stars and created us so that He might be able to love us and so that we might be able to love Him!"

Mark glanced out of the corner of his eye, watching Daniel's carefully molded presentation at his side. They labored in a flowing unison, English to Swahili, motion for motion, a swirling message of hope in two languages echoing across the valley. He was now aware of more movement; additional people edging their way up the hillside, creating an ever-growing crowd of seekers.

He told them of man's decision to go his own way and how sin had separated creation from loving Creator. He told of man's vain attempts to reach God, making sure that they realized that the sacrifices beneath that very tree had been similar exercises in futility. He spoke of God's step across the line, sending His only Son to pay a price for man that he could never pay for himself. He told them of the rough tree fashioned by man upon which God's Sacrifice was nailed for their sakes; of how God's power raised His Son Jesus from the grave on the third day, and how they could come to forgivness and life through faith in Him.

The people stood in rapt attention, their loose garments flowing gently in the cool breeze that was now beginning to blow across the rock-encircled plain. Mark became aware of the Masai warriors, moving closer, cutting their way through the crowd. Finally, as he began to invite people to life in Christ, the warriors, one after the other, began to kneel before the tree.

Others were responding to the invitation, stepping around the huddled figures. "This isn't happening," a voice

whispered to Mark's racing mind. "The Masai don't respond
... they don't accept what they consider to be the new ways!"
He feared that they didn't understand; that he had in some
way not been clear in the message.

Some of the African Pastors knelt with the hulking
men, placing their arms tentatively around their broad
muscled shoulders. So many times Mark had seen natural
enemies woven together in love at the foot of the cross.

As the counseling continued, the warriors were taken
aside and prayed with further. Hundreds of people had now
gathered on the hillside, kneeling, praying, being counseled in
the scattered shade of the tree.

"Bwana, this is an amazing day!" Tears were rolling
freely down Daniel's smiling face. "These Masai have come to
receive Jesus as Lord of their lives. God's joy has entered
them, and they are planning to return home to tell their
people."

"Do they truly understand?"

"Oh, yes Bwana! They understand!"

"I was afraid ... "

"They understood God's voice to their hearts, Bwana."
Daniel laughed. "Aren't you glad that He doesn't depend on
our abilities alone to touch people?"

Mark returned the smile. How glad he was that the
ultimate results rested in stronger hands than his. Soon these
noble men would return to Masai Mara. The Gospel would be
carried by them to the wild Serengeti Plains, to an age-old
culture nestled in scattered villages amidst flat-topped acacia
trees watered by the Mara River and its tributary the Talek
River.

A preacher from America, speaking a timeless message

through a translator from Kenya, was being used to set the stage for a movement of God's Spirit on the hearts of men who would carry that same message of hope into the fartherest corner of Africa.

"What a mighty God we serve," Mark hummed just beneath his breath. "What a mighty God we serve!"

Love Song

*T*he Mathre Valley simmered beneath the boiling equatorial sun. A hot wind whipped the fine dust that covered the field upon which the crusade site had been erected, stinging the eyes of people and animals alike. The herds of goats had been shooed to the outer perimeter, and the last of the decaying animal remains had been thrown into the open sewers that separated the site from the jumbled mass of primitive shanties. There, in structures constructed from rusting metal, broken wood and baking clay, thousands of families huddled somewhere between life and death.

Less than a mile from the site stood the towering hotels and businesses of modern Nairobi, and a few short miles past that, zebras and giraffes roamed freely, reminding all of the once wild heritage of a country that was now fitfully moving into the "modern" age.

Kent had been worried about this service. The choir from the local church had come to sing, bouncing excitedly on the crude platform that had been constructed only hours before. Colorfully dressed, beating drums and jangling tamborines, they had sung God's praises to the delight of the growing crowd packed tightly within the field. The national pastors, freshly trained at the Pastor's Conference at Limuru, wandered through the crowd, witnessing above the blaring music, handing out Swahili tracts and praying with some who had already given their hearts to Christ.

The service was running long, and Kent glanced continuously at his watch, all the while watching the sun that was now racing across the sky. There was always much to do after the service, and everything had to be packed up and out before nightfall.

He stepped onto the platform, balancing himself behind the two young Africans pastors who had finished leading the people in more singing. A moment later one of the American team members began to give his testimony, mimicked closely by one of their finest translators.

Kent stood silently, allowing his eyes to sweep across the sea of expectant faces before him. Torn, dusty, worn by weather and circumstances, the faces were open, their eyes latched on those who had come to share God's message.

His search stopped, however, as he caught a glimpse of a small boy, standing alone in the shadows; his leathery feet bare and dirty, his thin legs only slightly sheathed in patched pants sizes too large for his diminished frame. His hand was cupped over the side of his face, but Kent could still see the ravages of disease there. Most of his check had been eaten away, exposing reddened, bleeding gums.

Flies.

Thousands of them seemed to be swarming around the boy's head, trying to land on the wound. The boy habitually brushed them away, blinking his big, bright eyes.

His lips were moving.

"What is he saying?" Kent didn't realize that his mental questioning had erupted through his lips.

"What Bwana?" His translator bent toward him, seeking to better hear above the sound erupting from the speakers nearby.

"Do you see that boy?" Kent pointed toward the sunbaked buildings nearby. "There . . . in the shadows."

"Yes, Bwana. A boy." Why so much attention for a single boy? Didn't they come by the hundreds? Weren't they like the particles of dust that swirled around them? Thousands of children . . .

"His face . . . "

"Yes, Bwana. He has a sickness that is eating him away."

Kent turned and grasped his dark companion's arm. "Go down and listen to him. Come and tell me what the boy is saying."

He watched the African pastor's retreat. His comrade drew close to the boy, stood for a long moment, and then began to walk back toward the platform. Even from that distance Kent could see the tears coursing down the man's cheeks.

"What is he saying?"

The translator wiped the tears from his cheeks, ducking his head for a moment to regain his composure. "Oh, Bwana. He isn't saying anything. He's . . . singing."

"Singing?"

"Yes, Bwana. He's singing . . . ."

> *Jesus loves me . . . this I know . . .*
> *for the Bible tells me so.*
> *Little ones to Him belong . . .*
> *They are weak, but He is strong.*

Kent felt his own tears welling up around his eyes. A hurting child singing of a simple faith. Oh, how humbling an experience it always was. To watch Jesus move on the hearts and lives of His precious children.

> *Jesus loves the little children . . .*
> *All the children of the world.*
> *Red and yellows, black and white . . .*
> *they are precious in His sight.*
> *Jesus loves the little children of the world!*

Blind Allegiance

T he Southern Highlands of Tanzania are a lush wondrous locale. Past the city of Mbeya, nestled in a gap between the Mbeya mountain range to the north and the Uporoto Mountains to the Southeast, at the end of pitted trails that wind through divergent crops of rice, bananas, oranges, coffee and tea, can be found a sprinkling of small villages hidden from the prying eyes of the world.

After setting up a base of operations in the town of Tukuyu, the team from America had trained over 300 national pastors and evangelists for a week before beginning a divergent crusade ministry in the surrounding area.

They had traveled for what seemed hours, winding their way through fields, edging around mud-bogs and wrestling through dense walls of tangled undergrowth. Jason had just about given up. The promised crusade site was always supposedly just beyond the next ridge, or around the next bend, or secreted just across the next mud-thick field.

"Are you sure we're on the right path?" His question mirrored his growing apprehension.

The African driver smiled, reaching forward with a rag to once again wipe the thick dust from the windshield of the mile-beaten Land Rover. "Yes, Bwana. We're almost there. The journey is easier this time of the year. You should see it during the rainy season!"

Jason chuckled, and then realized that he wasn't kidding. He had been told that certain regions usually expected over 120 inches of rain each year. He silently agreed. No matter how bad it was . . . it could, he was sure, be much worse.

The trail widened, now edged with scattered people. Boys gingerly herded cattle and goats while women could be seen coming from all directions, carrying everything from pots and buckets to tree stumps upon their heads.

"We're almost to the village," his guide said. "It's a Market Day. Some of these women carry their load for hours just to trade for a sack of salt. They won't get back home until late in the night."

Jason fleetingly thought of his impatience while waiting in a seemingly long line at a grocery store before his departure from America.

"We can set up in the football field." The driver pointed to the right, outlining a broad plain of thick grass. Jason reminded himself that "football" meant something much different to most of the world. They knew nothing of helmets adorned with Viking warriors and bucking Broncos.

"We call it soccer," he whispered. He knew that the driver really didn't care.

Having staked out a crusade site, they began the process of gathering a crowd. Jason slipped to the sidelines, listening to the music and examining the inquisitive expressions on the sea of faces.

A hand tugged on his jacket sleeve. "Bwana, the pastor of the neighboring area is here. He'd like to meet with you."

Jason swung around, anticipating the proposed audience. "I'll take you to him," the man continued. He turned and led Jason past the perimeter of the site, out across the field and into a grove of trees. There, positioned against a sheltering tree, sat a man in his fifties, balding, dressed neatly in a tattered brown suit. His shoes were scuffed, beaten by the long march through rough terrain that had brought him to that location.

"I am Morris Jumbe," his guide explained. I am a Deacon at our church." He motioned toward another figure, standing afar off, a tattered Bible in his hand. "This is Dixon. He's a Deacon as well." He grabbed Jason's hand, leading him to the solitary figure sitting in the shadows.

"This is our pastor," he said proudly. Jason stepped forward, extending his hand. There was no response.

"I greet you in the Name of Lord Jesus," the pastor said with a glowing smile. "You'll forgive me for not coming to greet you personally. I'm blind, you see."

Jason lowered his hand, searching the man's dark eyes for any sign of life. There was none.

"You've met my Deacons. They lead me about my rounds. Usually it's just to the houses of our members and to the bedside of the sick and dying. But . . . today . . . they led me to this great Crusade!"

Jason turned questioningly. "You men lead your pastor everywhere he goes?"

"Yes," Morris Jumbe smiled. "It's our honor to be his eyes. Each day we lead him about so that he can do his work as God's minister."

"How far do you go each day?"

"Usually only a few miles," the man explained. "Today we had to begin a little earlier. We live about ten miles from here."

"Why . . . ?" He was embarrassed that he felt it neces-
sary to pursue the matter.

"We are God's servants as well. Our pastor has been
called of God to preach the Gospel and care for the church.
We are his eyes . . . we give ourselves to the work of God and
to the aid of our pastor."

Jason's mind ran back to the description of Deacons as
they had been called out for service in the First Century
church. He mentally added the phrase . . . "Humble servants
of God who lead their blind pastor about his appointed
rounds, sharing the love of God and contributing tirelessly to
the building up of God's church."

It sounded right.

The Appointment

Mombasa, the largest port on the coast of East Africa, serves as a dock and source of supply for not only Kenya, but also Uganda, Rwanda, Burundi and eastern Zaire. An ancient city, its history can be traced back to at least the 12th century, serving as an outpost for seafaring adventurers and cutthroats alike.

Although it is large in population, it has retained much of the "old world" flavor and character, with the Old Town between the Portugese-built Fort Jesus and the old docks remaining much as it was a hundred years ago.

Although normally steaming and hot so close to the equator, the team from America had found the weather to be quite pleasing, perhaps because most of them had chipped their way from an icy winter at home to make the journey.

The population, mostly Muslim, was going through a great time of unrest. The Pastor's Conference had been a successful time of sharing and training. However, when it came time to preach the crusades, it was discovered that the permits to hold such meetings in public had been canceled. Much unrest amidst Christian gatherings had brought about the edict, and it was left to God alone for resolution.

After negotiation it had been determined that crusades would be allowed on an "unofficial basis."

"You know why you are here, and so do we . . ." The District Commissioner explained the ground rules carefully. "You may set up wherever you see fit. But, I caution you. If there is trouble, we don't know you and we accept no responsibility."

It sounded, for a moment, like the opening scene of the old MISSION IMPOSSIBLE television program. *"If you accept this assignment . . . we will disavow all knowledge . . ."* The strategy was simple. No service would be announced in advance, the teams would set up and conduct the services as quickly as possible, and they would not return to the same location twice. In this way, it was hoped that the marauding, knife-wielding youth gangs that had been infiltrating Christian services would be kept off guard and held at bay.

It was against this unique backdrop that Brad found himself caught in what he perceived to be a trap. He had made what he now considered to be a rash promise to an African pastor. He had promised to minister in the same area for two days in a row.

"Yesterday wasn't too bad," his music man cajoled. "I couldn't believe it when the leader of that Mosque let us plug into his electrical outlet."

"Yea, setting up the platform by the mosque was . . . 'unique' . . . alright. I guarantee that they won't let it happen again tomorrow."

The site of the crusade had been exactly what Brad didn't want. Set far from the beaten path, they had ministered to a fractured line of pedestrians hurriedly moving toward work and nearby shops. Buses fitfully fumed on the street, bands of people edged by, and few stopped long enough to hear the music, let alone the message that he had preached from the back of the truck.

"I wish I hadn't made a promise to this guy," he smiled.

"There are lots of better places than this to draw a crowd. If there were any way out of it . . . I wouldn't show!"

Even as he said it, he knew that he would be keeping his word. He would take his team back to the same location, set up, and at least go through the motions.

"I wish we could find a garbage dump," he laughed. How well he remembered the first crusade they had preached. Unable to find another location, they had positioned their truck atop a jumbled garbage dump. The people from all the homes around had come, drawn first by the music and then by God's Spirit. When he had given the invitation, over 300 people had stepped forward, many of them kneeling in the debris, praying with tears to accept Jesus as Lord.

Brad had been deeply touched, and longed to see God move in a similar fashion again. He, however, doubted that he would see it cramped in the shadows of his current location.

As expected, the Mosque electricity wasn't available for their use the following day. They pulled out all of their power cords, assembling them into a pile.

"Gene, you take the cords and go down the street," he whispered to his comrade. "Find somebody who'll let you plug in and then bring us some power."

"I don't know," Gene laughed. "I've got about eight extension cords here . . . but I don't know how far it'll take us!"

"It'll have to be far enough." Brad watched him disappear down the street, finally veering into a series of crude shops huddled tightly against the hazy horizon. Many long minutes later he could be seen returning, stringing varied cords carefully behind him.

"Get the amplifier cord over here," he called. They stretched it as far as they could, mentally trying to measure the distance left to be traversed. Finally, Gene returned, the final dusty cord in his hand.

"Perfect!"

Brad wouldn't have believed it if he hadn't seen it for himself. Not one inch left to spare . . . exactly . . . positively . . . enough cord to make the connection.

"How are you going to tell them about that when you get back home?" Gene laughed, amused by the blank stare on his pastor's face.

"I'm going to let you do it," Brad grinned. "It's part of your assignment . . . you tell them about the 'Miracle Cord Connection'."

The music began playing, the African church members began witnessing to small huddled groups of people, and Brad prepared to once again hoist himself onto the truck, seeking to share good news with the people rushing past their location.

It appeared to be a carbon copy of the day before. Scattered sojourners, rumbling buses and trucks, and little opportunity to make a difference. "It's the last time I promise anyone something like this," he whispered to himself as he began to preach. The message was simple, as always. It told of a God who created everything, of man's rebellion that brought separation, and of God's initiative in sending His Son to provide a way of escape.

He was about two-thirds into the message when it happened. Brad would never be able to express it adequately in words. Years later he would still be left puzzled and speechless, trying to describe the experience.

It was like a transparent canopy descended over the scene. The harsh sounds of the street faded, the action shifted slowly into another speed, and a hush fell over everything. Brad stopped, unsure whether or not he should continue.

"What's that?" Gene ran around the truck, his eyes filled with a mixture of expectancy and surprise.

"It's the quiet," Brad breathed. He turned, now startled by the presence of the group that had instantly gathered before him. About fifty traditionally clad Muslims stood before the platform, seemingly frozen. Others stood beside the road, all eyes and attention focused on the preacher from the other side of the world.

Brad began to preach again, quickly drawing the sermon to a conclusion and a brief invitation to step forward and accept Jesus as Lord. All of the people crowded forward, many weeping, others falling to their knees in prayer. The pastor and his people moved forward, offering counsel and praying with those taking their stand for Christ.

Many who broke ranks and came would be ostracized by their families, or lose their livelihood, while some would even face threat of physical harm or death. It's hard to be a "middle of the road" Christian in the heart of Muslim culture. The people had counted the cost, and evidently discovered that Jesus was worth anything that might be required.

Brad stepped down from the truck, clasping Gene's cold hand.

"You have to tell them about this one," Gene laughed. Brad nodded ascent, although he knew that he wouldn't be able to. He did know one thing however. He knew that he had been taught a great lesson that would never be forgotten.

There are no "back alleys" and "second rate locations" when you're involved in the work of God's Kingdom. God moves where He chooses, and His purposes often defy the wisdom and short-sighted plans of mortal man. No, everyplace the Gospel is proclaimed, whether in the spotlight or the shadows, is destined to become, because of His presence, true holy ground.

School Days

*T*he pages of Tanzania's history are filled with vivid characters, clashing cultures and broad political strokes. Once a haven for Portuguese and Arab traders, the primitive villages had given up countless thousands to the slave trade; lost souls captured and transported from the main depots at Ujiji on the shores of Lake Tanganyika to Bagamoyo for final disposition at Zanzibar.

The British entered the scene early in the 19th Century, and worked for years seeking to undermine the slave trade activities. It was, however, the Germans that established colonialism in the area. The growth of the German East Africa Company soon led to the Germans taking Tanganyika, Rwanda and Burundi as protectorates while the British maintained Kenya and Uganda.

The Germans retained control until after World War One when the League of Nations mandated Tanganyika to the British and Rwanda and Burundi to the Belgians. In 1953, Julius Nyerere began a smooth bloodless transition that ultimately brought independence and combined Tanganyika with Zanzibar and the island of Pemba to form the United Republic of Tanzania.

Since the country was largely ignored and weakened by the British, added problems ultimately led the Tanzanians into Socialism in 1967. Based on the Chinese Communist model, the local villages were intended to be socialist organizations, created by the people and governed by the people who lived and worked there. The People's Republic of China moved in and built the TAZARA railway from the capital of Dar es Salaam to Kapiri Mposhi in Zambia.

Ultimately, however, the transportation system fell into ruin and the once bold experiment in radical socialism started to unravel at the core. It was into a battered, weakened country that a group of ministers from America traveled. They had come to sponsor a Conference For National Pastors and Evangelists, and would then take the trained (and hopefully inflamed) men into the field to teach them first-hand crusade evangelism and the techniques of effective one-on-one sharing of the Gospel.

"You're going to be speaking in the schools this week," the translator smiled. "We will see many of the young people respond to God's love!"

Ted pushed his Bible aside, trying to make the rapid transition from his sermon preparation to the conversation already in progress.

"What kind of schools?"

"It is the school of the older children . . . in your country, they'd be called Jr. and Sr. High students."

"What will we be allowed to do?"

"What you came to do!" Judson looked surprised at the question. Tall, dressed in a third generation pin-stripe suit, only his wrinkled face suggested that he was an older man. Ted had wished many times already that he had gotten in better shape, just so he could begin to keep up with his African counterpart.

"Preach?"

"You can preach . . . you can give out the New Testaments . . . you can witness . . ."

"Are these private schools?"

"No, of course not! These are government schools. You forget where you are, Bwana!"

Ted rolled the news around in his mind. Was such a thing possible? So much freedom. He'd believe it when he actually saw it.

The school was a rustic series of buildings, low, dirty, assembled in a circle around a barren yard. The students were already assembling by the time the van pulled into the complex. They had pulled their desks and affixed seats into long rows, and were now settled quietly awaiting their arrival.

The director of the school smiled warmly, welcoming Ted and the team. "You may set up your sound system here," he directed. "Our students have been anxious for your arrival."

Within minutes the equipment had been assembled, and Ted took the microphone in hand. They had brought several footballs (soccer balls in America) to present to the schools. It was amazing how much such items were prized. Each school leader acted like they had been presented with a new bus or something.

"We're glad to be here today at your school," he began. "I want to present you with a special gift from our team." He motioned for the director to join him on the platform perched atop the pickup bed. "This football will remind you of us. We give it gladly and hope that you'll enjoy it."

The school master's face gleamed as he received the ball and held it aloft amidst the applause and shouts of approval from both students and faculty.

"We accept it gladly," the man smiled. "We also welcome you and your message." He retreated, leaving Ted and his comrades to share the Gospel. For over forty-five minutes they sang and preached. Finally, amidst the familiar strains of "Just As I Am," students and teachers filed forward together to receive Jesus gladly as Lord.

"I will spend some time teaching my students from the Bible each day," one teacher said. "I have been a Christian for many years, and I have been praying that the Gospel would come to our children. I've shared my faith, and now you have come to tell them of God's love again. I promise that I'll help these students grow as Christians!"

As the counseling was being completed, Ted retreated, still trembling from the heartfelt response to the Gospel. Another African, neatly dressed, stood beyond the perimeter of the field, a glowing smile on his face. He stepped forward, his hand extended.

"I am Joseph Mwambe," he offered. "I am the official representative of the Government of Tanzania in this area."

Ted shook his hand warmly, surprised by the official presence.

"Your people are open to God's Word," Ted stuttered.

The man smiled broadly. "Yes, they are open to your message. Our children are our future. We are proud of them!"

Ted allowed his eyes to sweep the crusade site once again. National pastors praying with groups of children; teachers on their knees, giving their hearts to Christ while others were praying for wisdom to teach their students about the truths revealed in God's Word.

"Can I ask you something?" Ted found himself forging forward, seeking a solution to a mystery that had been plaguing him throughout the week.

"Of course," the official smiled. "That's why I'm here. We want you to feel welcome, and we want your questions answered."

"Why are we being allowed to do this?"

"What?" A look of surprise spread across his face.

"You allow us to come into your schools. We are allowed to hand out Bibles. I am allowed to preach and then give an invitation for your students and their teachers to accept the message of the Bible. Why are we being allowed to do this?"

"Why wouldn't you be?" The question sounded sensible, especially in this environment. "I'll say this," the man continued. "We have been watching Christians in our country for years. They are good people. They care for their children. They work hard and they are good citizens. They enrich us as a people and make us better." He smiled even more broadly. "Christians are good for our country. If we could . . . we'd help you make Christians of all our people!"

Ted turned and walked back toward the now dispersing assembly. A government taking note of the witness and lifestyle of God's people. Seeds of Christian living planted for years so that a government might see the need of God's message. Surely this was the mighty power that had shaken Imperial Rome to its very foundation centuries before.

Once the Amphitheatres of Rome had been considered the center of all power. The bright banners danced in the wind above the massive structures, the hot Mediterranean sun reflected off the polished armor of the world's greatest army, and the howl of a massive crowd drowned out all other sounds within a radius of miles. If you had been there, you might have shared in the misconception.

To find the real power, however, you would have had to descend to the lower chambers beneath the pomp. There, chained in dank dark cells, were the people of God, kneeling before their Lord, awaiting an uncertain fate on the blood-stained sand of the arena.

The might of Rome is gone today. The banners no longer fly in the breeze, the mighty army no longer marches, and the crowds no longer chant for the blood of the innocents in the broken arcades. Yet . . . the faith that lived in the hearts of those people imprisoned in the pit is as alive and dynamic as ever before! Principalities and powers come and go; conquerers assemble their armies and march them across the blood-stained pages of time, and then they are forgotten. Above it all stands the eternal God and His purposes.

God's truth outlives the vaulted philosophies and societies of men. If civilization and governments are to be changed, it must take place within the heart. That is the essence of the Great Commission. Change society by changing man from the inside out.

How is such a thing accomplished? As in Tanzania, by Christians demonstrating their faith before the world in which they live.

"This little light of mine . . . I'm gonna' let it shine!"

The Frog Prince

*J*oseph squinted, taken off guard by the sunlight flooding through the crude window above his head. He tried to move, rocking his body back and forth, until he was able to lean precariously against a rough bench nearby.

His body, warped from birth, had always been a burden, but it seemed even more so with the coming of adulthood. As a child his brothers and sisters had carried him everywhere, propping him against trees so that he could watch the other children at play. His mother had always hovered nearby, keeping watch over her crippled baby, making sure that no danger would befall him.

As childhood years gave way to maturity, however, he had been faced with the need to escape from the tender trap of his family. So, he had forced himself to walk, perching himself on his bleeding toes, waddling along like a skittering spider across the floor.

"More like a frog," his companions had said. "He squats and leaps like a frog!" The analysis of his appearance and manner of walking was usually cackled amidst harsh laughter.

Everyone had been surprised when a woman had consented to be his wife, and were even more astonished as they began to have a family of their own. Their shabby shanty became a home, and love dwelt there. This had been intensified by their embrace of Christianity, carried to them by loving church people from the nearby village.

The greatest astonishment had been voiced when he yielded to God's call to preach the Gospel. Since no one would entrust him with a church, he had begun his own and soon was the pastor of three congregations, and shuffled through the undergrowth each week to preach at four more far-flung preaching points.

Joseph looked around him, listening to the snoring of the other pastors reclining across the hard cement floor. They had, no doubt, sacrificed greatly to come the many miles to the Conference. Some had ridden for days on fuming buses, while many more had simply walked, carrying their dust-shrouded knapsacks with them. All had received an invitation from Jimmy Hodges through the Baptist General Convention of Tanzania. All had prayed, decided to grasp the once-in-a-lifetime training offered, and all had left family and friends behind to sleep on a floor and study God's Word on a hill-side in Tukuyu.

Those who had walked, however, had been able to do so upright. Those who rode buses had been able to sit on thin cushioned seats, rather than being stuffed awkwardly in a corner along with the luggage. Joseph, however, had never looked another man in the eye. He lived in a world of dirty feet and knees, always craning his neck so that he could see those who towered over him.

His diligence to his calling had won the respect of the others. They had come running to him as he waddled up the hill toward the conference grounds, pushing himself along on the crude blunt wooden stilts he had made to protect his hands.

"Welcome, Joseph!" They had meant it, gladly receiving him as an elder statesman of the faith. They had heard of the attempts on his life; of the poison meant for him that had swept his beloved wife close to the doors of death instead. The enemies of the Gospel feared him and his commitment, and they had tried, without success, to end his life on many occasions.

"God's goodness has brought me here," he had cried as he accepted their embrace. The wonder was that he meant it. In spite of his terrible crippled frame, God had granted him life, a family and an opportunity to participate in things that would last forever.

"I'll get a new body soon enough," he had told his wife before beginning the long painful journey. "But I think God expects me to wear this one out for Him first!"

A bell clanged outside, the first call to another day of worship and learning. The team from America had labored long, teaching each of the men about everything from witnessing and pastoral skills to the development of a personal devotional life. Most of the pastors had never been trained in any way before, and they hovered in the classes like baby birds, ready to pounce on any morsel of wisdom or experience.

He pulled himself slowly across the floor, groaning slightly above the yawns and awakening voices of his comrades. It had become a life-long routine. Starting early so that he could lead others, or at least stay out of their way.

The classes, led by preachers and teachers from the United States, were designed to give a wide range of training to men who had received little in the past. It was the Witnessing Class, however, that began to stir memories in Joseph's heart. He was reminded anew of God's grace that had reached down to touch him.

"He had to reach further down than usual," he had laughed to his friends. "Saul of Tarsus had to be stricken to the ground . . . I was born with my nose in the dirt already."

He had even been surprised when God had called him to preach. How could he? There were so many needs . . . so many far-flung pockets of people hungering for the Gospel message. Men with good straight legs had buckled under the load. How would a groveling cripple delve into the thicket, searching out seeking hearts and hurting lives?

Beginning slowly, he had begun preaching in one area after another, establishing churches and then pressing ever outward, seeking to bring God's promises to more and more of his countrymen.

As he sat in the classes, however, he was impressed that he still hadn't done enough. The Scriptures kept reeling through his brain, calling him onward in search of greater spiritual conquests.

> *"For you see your calling, brethren, that not many wise according to the flesh, not many mighty, not many noble, are called."*

He remembered the initial laughter that had greeted his coming into an area, ultimately transformed into a hush as he had spoken of God's promises that could be theirs.

> *"But God has chosen the foolish things of the world to put to shame the wise, and God has*

*chosen the weak things of the world to put to
shame the things which are mighty; and the
lowly things of the world and the things
which are not, to bring to nothing the things
that are, that no flesh should glory in His
presence."*

He remembered how the crowds had thanked God for
His promises, and how all had rejoiced that such a crippled
messenger had been sent. If God could use him, the people
reasoned, then He could use them all. If God loved this lowly
man, then He surely loved them all!

"He who glories, let him glory in the Lord."

It was almost the end of the conference before the re-
alization came. He still hadn't done enough. He had pushed
out further than most others, had undergone ridicule and
devious attacks on his life, and yet he still wasn't doing
enough. There was no way that he could possibly repay the
love debt he owed to God. While all others had despised him,
God had loved him and sent His Son to pay the price for his
sins. When no other would give him respect, God had called
him from the ranks to be His messenger, allowing him to
carry the most important message in the universe to his own
people.

"I must do more," he whispered to a nearby comrade.

The man seemed perplexed, searching for words. "How
can you do that? How can you go further?"

"I must start earlier, and I must stay later," he smiled.
"There are some villages that are untouched, tucked deeply

in the shadows of the Livingstone Mountains. God loves those people and I must take His word to them."

After the Conference, Joseph shuffled down the dusty hill, often turning to wave a callused hand at departing friends from both his own land and beyond. He pulled himself methodically forward, coughing amidst the dust that flew thickly into his face.

He was smiling. He was renewed. There were still mountains to climb for God's glory . . . even for a man who had never had the opportunity to stand.

Four

Malawi Journal

"Miles To Go Before I Sleep . . . ."

*T*he 747-300 has settled quietly into the long night, finally lulling most of the passengers into fitful slumber. They have been fed, entertained and cajoled by a company of professionals working feverishly to make the ten hour flight from Los Angeles to Amsterdam as painless as possible.

The overhead video screen flickers out the monotonous information: Ground speed 595 mph, altitude 33,000 feet, outside temperature minus 75 degrees F. Cutting upward through the heart of the United States, the plane has soared above the Grand Canyon, Casper and Fargo, edging its way across Greenland toward its eventual drop over Scotland.

This is when the melancholy sets in. Every time I go it seems I have more to leave behind. The woman that I've spent 30 years of my life with, my children and their spouses, and a growing crop of grandchildren. I know that if it weren't for my conviction of the world's lostness, I would never again leave those so dear to me to streak through this black night to the far side of the planet. When I draw my final breath, I won't be remembering great adventures and exotic travels. I may, however, somehow regret the days that I didn't spend with my wife, my children and their children.

The Apostle Paul said that if Christ isn't risen from the grave, we are the saddest and most pathetic of all creatures.

Perhaps he meant that it costs a lot to believe and share this faith. More than we can afford, if our message is any less than the greatest truth in the universe.

> *The woods are lovely-dark and deep*
> *but I have promises to keep.*
> *and miles to go before I sleep,*
> *miles to go before I sleep.*

"Further Into The Night . . . ."

T he plane rocks languidly, gorged with darkness, sprinkled with sporadic points of yellowed light. Stone black dignitaries from African nations, their three piece suits nicely pressed and shoes rubbed to a glowing shine. Europeans on holiday, businessmen on their appointed rounds, and other weary travelers tucked into the shadows, strapped together amidst the whir of the engines and a sea of whispered conversations, an intertwining chorus of conflicting languages and dialects.

Sprinkled throughout is the God-picked team that is being sent to Malawi. I am always surprised. Incredibly diverse in background, talent and personality, they are even now being woven together into a tapestry of service.

It's always the same. No one would put such a group together on purpose, yet they are all perfect parts of the puzzle. One of the greatest miracles of each project is seeing what the Lord has in mind. He never makes mistakes in the personnel department.

"Our Destination"

We come to Lilongwe, the capital of Malawi. Named after the river that flows from the nearby Dzalanyama Hills, it became officially known as the new capital of the country in 1975. A rapidly growing area, it is home to over 325,000 souls.

We have lost two nights sleep on the journey, and now begin the 5 hour drive down the thin trunk of the country to our final destination — Blantyre.

Named after the birthplace of missionary explorer Dr. David Livingstone, the city came into existence as a mission site on October 23, 1876 when it was founded by missionaries of the Established Church of Scotland.

The city nestles comfortably amidst a grouping of hills and mountains: Michiru, the "rain mountain"; craggy Chirandzula; and Ndirande, the "sleeping man mountain." It is the "big city" of Malawi, and our ministry will be at the heart of its half million plus inhabitants.

Arriving in the blackness, we unload, eat, sing and share together before retiring to the first bed we have seen in days. The dawn will bring the opportunity we have come seeking, and only God Himself knows what lies in wait.

"The Pastors Arrive . . ."

*T*hey come toward the conference, a snaking line of men drawn by the promise of training and fellowship. Down the Ml from mountainous towns like Dedza; Down from the spine of the Shire Highlands, from Zomba and Blantyre's suburb of Limbe; from the emerald green tea plantations of Thyolo, Mulanje and Chilwawa, or the Sucoma sugar plantations at Nehalo.

Their suit coats dusty from the journey, their shoes worn and tattered by miles of travel. They carry their thin cloth bags, stuffed to overflowing with clothes. Many grasp Bibles in their hands, waving them triumphantly as they yell words of greeting and praise to God.

After registration they are given their conference packets and supplies, assigned rooms and issued mattresses to sleep on.

"Muli Bwanji?" They greet you by asking if you are well.

"Ndili Bwano," you reply with a smile. They grasp your hand and shake it warmly. "Zikomo gwambile," they repeat over and over again. Their gratitude is honest, and their spirits warm and excited about the prospect of what God will be doing.

The first worship experience with the pastors was glorious! I've never heard anything like their singing. When you're there in person, you can feel it vibrate in your bones and can almost see electricity flashing through the air!

We gave them their Bibles. They danced and sang, holding the precious books toward Heaven. Many of these men have been preaching for years without a Bible of their own. We take so much for granted. I was, for a moment, ashamed to live in a land where God's Word is so available and so seldom read. It is embraced here like a thirsty man yearns for cool water. God forgive us!

I teach at the Conference today. I'll be leading five 50 minute sessions discussing the role of the church in the training of disciples. Thousands are going to be born into God's Kingdom in the days to come and it's vital that these men know how to lead their church to "grow" babes in Christ.

They move silently into the jumbled room. Tall, short, dust covered and tattered. Most wear old worn suits and jackets, their feet either encased in old scuffed shoes or simply bare and callused.

They clutch their new Bibles and notebooks tightly to themselves, as if fearing that someone might snatch the precious treasures from them.

My translator works in perfect union with me, shadowing my every motion and almost anticipating my every line. The men take hurried notes, leaning forward like hungry baby birds, reaching to be fed by their mother.

There is a holy quality to this scene. You can almost see them growing, and you receive immediate gratification as lights of recognition spark and flash behind their searching eyes.

These men are the hope of Central Africa. May God teach them, ignite them and send them boldly forth. I feel that I should slip off my shoes as well. This truly may be holy ground.

"Into The Harvest . . ."

*T*oday is the last day of the conference. This afternoon I will go on a bus with about 80 national pastors into our first crusade site. I'll get them organized and then send them out in pairs to share their faith. They have been taught in the classroom, and now it's time for their work in "the lab" among the people of the area.

The South Lunzu Market is a small collection of rude primitive buildings nestled at the foot of a range of rock-clustered mountains. The air hung thick with smoke and dust as the bus rattled onto a small clearing in the heart of the marketplace.

Within an hour the music was playing through the sound system and we were building a crowd. What power there is in the Gospel of Jesus Christ! It is always a wonder. You can see it in their eyes — that instant when God's Spirit drives the wondrous truth of hope and reconciliation into their hearts. God calls people to Himself, and those who listen respond to such a simple message.

Over 1,000 adults stepped forward to receive Christ when I gave the invitation. I've stood there so many times before, but it always takes my breath away. The glory of it all!

The pastors worked feverishly on the counseling. All decisions were carefully recorded so that the local churches can begin discipling.

Darkness enveloped us as we loaded the last of the equipment. The buses still weren't back to pick up the pastors. Finally, over an hour late, one of them limped into view. The slowly emerging story revealed that the second bus wouldn't be coming.

I was forced to make a series of decisions. I sent the bus back loaded with half of the pastors (along with one pastor to guard the driver and assure that he would return for the rest). I then sent the American team back in the van and decided to stay with the pastors and await the bus.

We stood together in the darkness, surrounded by flickering fires and covered with a bright canopy of stars not seen in Arizona. Beneath that strange sky we began to sing to the mountains. We sang to the glory of our God!

I glanced around, realizing that some of the pastors had surrounded me, protecting me from the cool breeze and any possible danger. Oh — how I love it! The simplicity, the power and the fellowship in Christ!

Much later in the night the bus returned for us. As we bumped toward "civilization" once again, the men sang with greater intensity and joy.

The service we were planning to attend was almost over when we arrived. The pastors unloaded and marched triumphantly down the aisle, praising God. Soon they were joined by the others, standing to their feet in celebration.

The bus problem was no surprise. Such things are expected and flexibility is the key ingredient when ministering in Africa. My dear friend, Ralph Bethea, used to exclaim "AWA!" It means — "Africa Wins Again!"

Perhaps. But Satan won nothing at the South Lunzu

market on this night. The angels rejoiced, the power fell and I sang with my brothers in an "unknown tongue" on a dark cool night on the far side of the world.

Who could ask for more?

"Peddle Into All The World . . ."

We drove into the grounds of the Baptist Center at 7:00 A.M. on Sunday morning. There, encircled by flowering trees and a line of smiling African pastors, was a vast collection of gleaming chrome. The bicycles, purchased through the giving of generous Christians in America, had been delivered. The men broke into jubilant song, praising God for His wondrous provision. There is no way to adequately describe their excitement.

Many of the men pastor seven or eight churches and travel to other preaching points as well. Some travel up to 25 miles just to reach their people. They will no longer walk. They will ride in style and spread the Gospel. After we are gone to be with Jesus many of these bikes will still be in service for the Lord.

One of the pastors has an annual income of less than $200.00 per year. He is married and the father of six children. This is, by far, the most valuable thing he will ever own.

I asked him, "What will you do with it? You pastor eight churches and travel to seven other preaching points. Will it be easier now?"

He smiled and replied, "Yes. Now I can REALLY start some more preaching points!"

So it is in Africa. You have made a wise investment that will still be paying dividends when Jesus comes!

"Crusade!"

*T*he crusaders of old brought nations to their knees by the power of the sword. They subjected the body, but didn't touch the soul. We have come with another sword — the Word of God. It slices to the quick of men's spirits, and transforms them forever from the inside out.

Sometimes in Market Places, often in villages, we set up our vehicles and equipment to share Good News. They come by the thousands, a swirling sea of humanity that surrounds us.

It would be so easy to simply begin to think of them as numbers — cold statistics to take home and share in America. But they are people — God created and God loved — and I always pick out three or four and watch them from the platform.

Sometimes they are young men, muscled from working in the fields; sometimes young mothers, a tiny child hung tightly upon her back; sometimes a businessman in neatly pressed suit and sunglasses. I watch their faces as I preach the Gospel. Sometimes they weep as they hear of God's love for them; sometimes they kneel or bow their heads, broken by the breath of God upon their hearts.

It is Wednesday and over 16,000 people have said "yes" to Jesus Christ. I'll go home and some will say, "Oh — that's nice!" What would they say if 16,000 accepted Jesus in Phoenix in five days? If they could look into the eyes of these people, they would realize that there's no difference at all. We are, quite simply, laboring in the fields of our Lord, and He is providing the strength, the message, the power and the increase!

"The Immensity Of It All!"

*I*t's Thursday night, and 24,000 people have been born into God's Kingdom during the crusade services this week. The mind can't comprehend it — I am numb. The Bible says that one soul is worth more than all the riches of the universe. We are dealing in quantities that boggle the imagination, and I can't understand why God is allowing us to even watch Him do such things.

I look into the faces of the people, remembering that any one of them was worth the blood of Jesus. It's bigger than we are, happening all around us. God's Spirit blowing like a wind, loving, drawing, cleansing, transforming.

I keep thinking that I'll have to go home and tell the people what I've seen. How will I do that? What new words will I have to invent?

How big is God?
How big and wide His vast domain?
To try to tell my lips can only start.
He's big enough to rule the mighty universe —
Yet small enough to live within my heart.

"Cry For The Children"

I cried today.

I didn't mean to. This afternoon I lowered my fortifications and walked among the children. I had told myself not to. I always go home seeing their faces in the night, and I had determined not to feel this time.

I shook their hands, I hugged them and I walked with them. Beautiful, friendly, haunting — the children of Africa.

A little baby girl was nestled tightly on the back of her mother. I stopped to greet her, and a look spread across her face. Tears began to well up in her big eyes and I realized that it was the look my precious granddaughter Erin gets when confronted by a stranger.

I cried today.

Another little girl, her fists firmly planted on her hips, was involved in getting several of the other children organized and just the way she wanted them. I suddenly realized that she had assumed the same stance my lovely granddaughter Ashleigh always assumes.

I cried today.

Many of these children will never grow old enough to love and have children of their own. A God of mercy has allowed us to come and touch them in His Name.

> *Jesus loves the little children —*
> *All the children of the world.*
> *Red and yellow, black and white —*

They are precious in His sight.
Jesus loves the little children of the world!

Cry for the children of Africa!

"Crusade Conclusion"

W e held our final crusade service in a small village setting just outside Blantyre. The women had gathered, jars and buckets on their heads, waiting to purchase water at the local well. Above them, outlined against an afternoon sky of deep blue, could be seen others washing their clothes and beating them on rocks.

Amidst this tranquil setting, in a small clearing, we set up our trucks and gave the service over to the nationals. They sang, witnessed and preached. A group of people stepped forward into life, we loaded up and returned to our lodging for much needed rest.

Over 30,000 people have come to receive Jesus as Lord this week — in addition to precious children — seemingly as many as the stars of the midnight sky. I can't fathom it all — and I've witnessed it firsthand. I don't expect you, dear reader, to grasp it. Just give God glory and believe in miracles!

"Harvest Thoughts"

*S*omeone might well ask, "Will all of these thirty thousands go on to be faithful disciples and fruitful Christians?" The answer, obviously, is "No." No more than
all those who followed Jesus while He walked the earth
remained faithful.

It's sorta like it was in Washington State when I was a
young man. I worked as a field hand in the apple harvest.
There were Extra Fancys, Fancys, Standards, C Grades and
Culls. Some were bound for the New York markets and some
were destined to be cider and apple sauce.

At the end of the day, I might have picked two bins of
apples. You could have asked me, "How many Fancys do you
have in the bin?" "How many culls did you pick today?" I
wouldn't be able to tell you. I'd say, "The boss does the grad-
ing and sorting. They are, after all, his apples. It's my job as
a field hand to get as much of the harvest as possible before
harvest time ends."

So it is in Africa today. I've done my best in the field,
trusting God alone for the increase. Now, each precious soul
is in His hands.

I will say one thing, however. Many Fancys have passed
by my vantage point this week, and God will be using them,
and more like them, to shake Malawi to its knees in the years
to come.

Faithfulness is what He requires. "*. . . the night is coming when no man can work.*"

"The Greatest Adventure"

*I*t's as though the United Nations has sent representatives from all nations to be sealed in a capsule and jettisoned through space at 600 miles per hour. Africans, East Indians, Scandanavians, Italians and Americans. We pass over places whose very names conjure up vivid visions of great adventure — Zanzibar, Nairobi, Casablanca and Algiers. Yet, no event recorded in secular history or created in the imagination could begin to match the adventure we have shared in the heart of Africa.

We, mere mortals, have been allowed to watch God do those things that He alone can do. Forgive sin — relieve guilt — restore homes — transform lives. It is the ultimate adventure — living in a "Bad News World" and having the opportunity to share "Good News."

Over 275 African leaders trained and inflamed — over 30,000 precious souls stepping forward into life in addition to countless children in whose hearts eternal seed has been planted.

Perhaps you'll join us next time. All that can be promised is hard work, high adventure and life-changing blessing! Pray about it! Let's accept life's greatest challenge — together!

Five

The Message

The Message

I made a mistake the first time I went to minister in Africa. I watched God move powerfully in the hearts of people. They stepped forward by the thousands driven by a seemingly childlike faith and a hunger for hope in their lives. My mistake was that I began to believe that it was "Africa." I had never seen people in my own land respond so freely, and so I almost believed that God somehow works differently on the other side of the world.

That, of course, isn't true. He is the same to all, and His power and message are not diminished or altered by geography. He is the same, the message is the same, and the result is the same. People who come to God through faith in Jesus Christ are forgiven, washed clean, made new, adopted into His family and given the promise of everlasting life. It isn't that God is speaking more in Africa. It's simply that people are listening more there.

The Bible says in Romans 3:23, *"For ALL have sinned and come short of the glory of God."*

ALL of us have missed the mark; we have fallen short of God's great purpose for us, and NO sin can stand in His Holy presence. This sin separates us from God and eternity.

Romans 6:23 says, *"The wages of sin is death, but the gift of God is eternal life through Jesus Christ our Lord."*

Sin pays off in death. Not just physical death, but spiritual death. We are alive to the world around us, but we are dead to God and the things of God in our natural state. I. Corinthians 2:14 states, *"The natural man receiveth not the things of the Spirit of God: for they are foolishness to him: neither can he know them, because they are spiritually discerned."*

God created us for Himself, but our sin and rebellion separated us from Him. We have no way of getting back to God on our own, so He initiated a plan which would open a door back to Himself. It would satisfy His righteousness by allowing sin to be judged, and it would also allow a way of forgiveness for us. He sent His only Son, Jesus Christ, to take the punishment of sin in our place.

John 3:16 says, *"For God so loved the world (that's you and me) that He gave His only begotten Son, that whosoever believeth in Him should not perish, but have everlasting life."*

The Bible says that to receive His sacrifice for ourselves, we need to repent (which means turning from our old direction away from God and beginning to seek His will for our lives) and receive His sacrifice by faith.

Jesus said Himself in John 5:24, *"Most assuredly, I say unto you, he who hears My word and believes in Him who sent Me has everlasting life, and shall not come into judgment, but has passed from death into life."*

At that moment, when we receive God's promise through Christ by faith, God by His Holy Spirit enters into our lives and begins the process of making us new. Our sins are forgiven, we are washed clean, and given the promise that we will spend eternity with Him. After you meet Jesus, you are not the same.

II. Corinthians 5:17 states, *"Therefore, if anyone is in Christ, he is a new creation; old things have passed away; behold, all things have become new."*

Romans 5:8 makes a great promise to us. *"God demonstrates His own love toward us, in that while we were still sinners, Christ died for us."* He is the one way to forgiveness, a relationship with God, and everlasting life. Acts 4:12 states it clearly. *"Nor is there salvation in any other, for there is no other name under heaven given among men by which we must be saved."*

Today, just like the seeking thousands in the heart of Africa, you can pray and ask God to make a difference in your life. He is willing to forgive, forget, cleanse and lead. You are the only one who can decide.

You can pray a simple prayer similar to the one below. Remember that prayer is not an expression of the lips. It is communication with God in our hearts. The words must express what you truly mean. You can pray like this . . .

"Dear God, I thank you for loving me. I confess that I am a sinner like everyone else, and I know that my sin separates me from You. I thank You for sending Your son Jesus, to die in my place and take the punishment for my sin. I want to turn and go Your way. Please forgive all of my sin. Jesus, come into my life right now, as You promised that You would do. Please lead me, make me into what You would have me to be, and give me the promised everlasting life. Thank You for doing what You promised. I pray this in Jesus' Name. Amen."

If you prayed this prayer and meant it, God now dwells

in you, your sins are forgiven, and you have eternal life. This is based, never on feelings or emotions, but on the fact that God promised that He would do it, and He never breaks His word.

Now, you need to share this most important of all decisions with someone else. Contact the pastor of a Bible preaching church. He will share with you how you can grow strong in your new spiritual life through the study of God's Word, the Bible, and the development of your communication with God through the wonderful gift of prayer.

You are now a part of a great world-wide family. It is comprised of countless people from the four corners of the earth who have been wise enough to make this decision for themselves as well. Welcome to the family! Don't stop now! The best is yet to come!

Other Books By Dale Freeman

Animal — The Gene Culver Story
Like Trees Walking
My Soul To Take
The Dinetah Tapes
The Dinetah Reunion
Congregation — A Dinetah Appendage
Distant Harvest
Cactus Cross
Animal 2 — Promises To Keep
The Last Summer
Cross Roads